Praise for *Peak Property Performance*

"Every commercial real estate professional needs this book. *Peak Property Performance* breaks down the critical elements of digital transformation and shows how to leverage AI and data for unmatched operational efficiency and profitability."

—Zain Jaffer, owner, Zain Ventures Family Office

"This isn't just another tech book—it's a masterclass in creating value through data and digital infrastructure. After implementing the OpticWise methodology at our 200-acre Aspiria campus, I can attest: These strategies work. Read this book before your competitors do."

—Chad J. Stafford, president,
Occidental Management, Inc.

"We're at a pivotal moment where data collection, analysis, and security converge to create unprecedented opportunities in real estate. This step-by-step guide reveals how to harness your building's digital potential, optimize operations, and create new revenue streams. The timing couldn't be better—and the cost of inaction couldn't be higher."

—Seth E. Konkey, vice president, Jacobs Solutions, Inc.

"This groundbreaking guide reveals how AI can transform affordable housing economics. Drawing from proven strategies, it shows developers how to cut costs and streamline operations while maximizing limited public and private capital. Essential reading for anyone serious about tackling housing affordability."

—Michael Egidi, CFA, Affordable Housing Investor

"Fifteen years ago, we bet big on data analytics when we built AMLI's first dashboard. I've seen firsthand how digital infrastructure separates market leaders from the competition. This book delivers the strategic framework and tactical guidance needed to implement a successful digital transformation. Don't wait to future-proof your portfolio."

—Fred Schreiber, executive vice president and COO, AMLI Residential

"After years of managing corporate real estate portfolios, I can tell you that digital infrastructure isn't just about efficiency—it's about transforming the tenant experience. This book reveals how innovative data & technology can create workplaces that attract and retain top talent while driving operational excellence. Essential reading for anyone serious about future-proofing their portfolio."

—Wyn Channer, senior managing director, JLL

"As a developer, general contractor, and operator of 4,000+ units, I know the challenges of implementing new technology across a portfolio. This book cuts through the hype to deliver a practical digital infrastructure framework that drives NOI. Whether you're developing new projects or optimizing existing assets, these strategies work."

—Joe Fielden Jr., vice president, JA Fielden Co., Inc.

"Witnessing PropTech's evolution across global markets, I can confirm: *Peak Property Performance* isn't just another tech manual—it's the definitive playbook for transforming real estate operations. Douglas and Hall's 5C Framework revolutionizes how we think about property optimization, showing leaders exactly how to harness AI and digital infrastructure for unprecedented returns. Essential reading for anyone serious about building a real estate dynasty in the digital age."

—Louisa Dickins, co-founder and director, LMRE

"Having guided multiple technologies from startup to billion-dollar exits, I can confirm that this book represents commercial real estate's next major value creation opportunity. Control of data and digital directly impacts NOI—creating immediate returns and competitive advantages. Bill's insights aren't theoretical—they're the blueprint for a significant edge in asset valuation and performance."

—Thomas Noonan, lead director of Intercontinental Exchange (ICE) and chairman, TEN Holdings

"One of the real estate industry's greatest arbitrages is digital infrastructure. Bill's playbook shows how to monetize your building's data streams to optimize operations and boost NOI. These strategies allow you to see buildings as data-driven assets, so you generate higher yields, establishing and maintaining sovereignty over your data, and locking in a meaningful competitive advantage."

—Kevin Choquette, founder, Fident Capital

"Douglas and Hall nail a crucial truth: Data transformation requires universal team buy-in. *Peak Property Performance* provides the perfect playbook for the cultural and strategic shifts needed in commercial real estate. While most books discuss AI theoretically, this one delivers practical steps tailored to our industry. As a CRE data scientist, I can confirm this is the roadmap we've been waiting for."

—Shea Fallick, CRE data scientist and product leader

"Finally, a blueprint that speaks to builders and developers about digital infrastructure without the tech jargon. *Peak Property Performance* offers concrete strategies for reducing new construction costs while future-proofing your buildings. The authors' real-world experience shines through in practical guidance that could save millions in CapEx on your next project. Essential reading before finalizing any new development plans."

—Vinny English, built environment expert and real estate developer

"This book is an eye-opener. It illustrates how to leverage AI and data for unmatched operational efficiency and profitability, provides a strategic framework, and outlines the tactical steps needed to implement a successful digital transformation. It changes how we see and operate buildings as data-driven assets and the importance and value of control of data."

—David P. Mead, president,
The Mead Consulting Group

"Having worked with numerous proptech founders with a combined market cap of $1.86B, I know what excellent and transformational looks like! Take it from me: Bill has the definitive roadmap for optimizing commercial real estate assets by re-imagining the legacy business models that CRE owners, investors, and operators have been using for decades, which leaves so many dollars on the table. Digital infrastructure, data ownership, and how to provide the finest UX for tenants are just some of the topics covered."

—Andrew Stanton, CEO, Proptech-X

"I've helped enterprises extract maximum value from their tacit digital assets for decades. *Peak Property Performance* elevates this concept for real estate, offering a proven formula for driving unprecedented returns from properties in new and fast ways using existing resources. Douglas's strategic framework transforms conventional CRE thinking, showing leaders how to leverage data and digital infrastructure to unlock hidden value quickly. A must-read for any executive seeking reliable, innovative paths to higher asset performance despite changes in the market."

—William C. Weiss, chairman
and CEO, The Promar Group, LLC

PEAK
PROPERTY
PERFORMANCE

PEAK
PROPERTY
PERFORMANCE

Game-Changing AI and Digital Strategies
for Commercial Real Estate

BILL DOUGLAS & DREW HALL

with RYAN R. GOBLE

FAST
COMPANY
Press

Fast Company Press
New York, New York
www.fastcompanypress.com

Distributed by Greenleaf Book Group

For ordering information or special discounts for bulk purchases, please contact Greenleaf Book Group at PO Box 91869, Austin, TX 78709, 512.891.6100.

Design and composition by Greenleaf Book Group and John van der Woude
Cover design by Greenleaf Book Group and John van der Woude
Joystick and magnifying glass icons © Adobe Stock / Darwin Mulya

Publisher's Cataloging-in-Publication data is available.

Print ISBN: 978-1-63908-128-8

eBook ISBN: 978-1-63908-129-5

To offset the number of trees consumed in the printing of our books, Greenleaf donates a portion of the proceeds from each printing to the Arbor Day Foundation. Greenleaf Book Group has replaced over 50,000 trees since 2007.

Printed in the United States of America on acid-free paper

25 26 27 28 29 30 31 32   10 9 8 7 6 5 4 3 2 1

First Edition

The way a team plays as a whole determines its success. You may have the greatest bunch of individual stars in the world, but if they don't play together, the club won't be worth a dime.

—**Babe Ruth,** seven-time World Series champion and one of baseball's greatest players, who revolutionized the game with his power hitting

If you go around being afraid, you're never going to enjoy life. You have only one chance, so you've got to have fun.

—**Lindsey Vonn,** Olympic gold medalist and the most successful American ski racer in history, with eighty-two World Cup victories

We all have dreams. But in order to make dreams come into reality, it takes an awful lot of determination, dedication, self-discipline, and effort.

—**Jesse Owens,** four-time Olympic gold medalist who shattered Adolf Hitler's myth of Aryan supremacy at the 1936 Berlin Olympics

Contents

Dorit Fischer

When Bill Douglas and Drew Hall approached me to write a foreword for *Peak Property Performance*, I recognized an opportunity to highlight what many in our industry need, but few have articulated: a practical framework for transforming commercial properties through data ownership and digital infrastructure.

As a broker who has spent over twenty years structuring complex deals in Denver's evolving neighborhoods, I've witnessed firsthand how value is created in commercial real estate. While location remains paramount, operational excellence increasingly separates market leaders from average performers. The gap between traditional operators and those leveraging technology for competitive advantage grows wider each year.

What excites me about this book is its laser focus on profitability. This isn't technology for technology's sake—it's a blueprint for increasing net operating income through smarter operations. The authors' 5C Framework transforms abstract concepts into actionable strategies that directly impact the bottom line.

In my work with clients ranging from housing authorities to private investors, I've learned that successful real estate strategies require understanding stakeholders' goals and finding creative solutions to complex challenges. The multilayered deals I've structured—like the historic Evans School transformation or the Johnson & Wales campus repositioning—succeed because they align diverse interests toward common objectives. This book applies similar principles to property operations, showing how aligned digital infrastructures and systems create exponential value.

For too long, commercial real estate has lagged behind other industries in leveraging data. Many owners surrender valuable information to vendors without realizing its worth or potential. The authors' emphasis on data ownership strikes me as particularly timely and important. The thinking captured in these pages represents a significant untapped asset for most property owners.

Throughout my career, I've enjoyed learning about "the functionality of business." I love understanding how companies operate and how their real estate needs support their missions. This book extends that concept. Douglas and Hall reveal how properties themselves function as operational businesses with optimization opportunities at every level. The fifty-five specific strategies they share in chapter four provide a creative list of immediate avenues for improvement across any portfolio and the basis for creativity far beyond what's listed.

Most compelling is how these strategies enhance rather than replace the human elements of our business. By automating routine tasks and focusing on finding deeper insights, running your properties with a focus on owning your data and digital infrastructure, property teams are freed up to focus on relationship building and creative problem-solving. These are the aspects of our work that genuinely create lasting value.

For those managing historic properties like the ones I've helped transact, these approaches offer ways to preserve architectural heritage while creating modern, efficient operations. For developers of new projects, they provide opportunities to build competitive advantages from the ground up. Regardless of your portfolio's composition, these strategies apply universally.

I believe we stand at an inflection point in commercial real estate. The next decade will reward those who embrace data-driven operations and penalize those who cling to outdated practices. *Peak Property Performance* provides the roadmap for positioning yourself on the right side of this divide—not just surviving industry transformation but leading it.

This isn't merely a technology book. It's a business strategy guide that happens to leverage data, digital, and technology as its primary tools. For anyone serious about maximizing returns in commercial real estate, it offers a practical, proven approach to achieving truly peak performance.

—Dorit Fischer
Partner, NAI Shames Makovsky

Zain Jaffer

Every commercial real estate professional needs this book. *Peak Property Performance* breaks down the critical elements of digital transformation and shows how to leverage AI and data for unmatched operational efficiency and profitability.

In the fast-moving world of commercial real estate, a technological revolution is quietly unfolding. Just as we witnessed digital transformation reshape industries from advertising to transportation, the buildings that form the backbone of our economy are now poised for their own evolutionary leap. But unlike disruptions that come from outsiders, this revolution offers unprecedented opportunity to those already within the industry—if they're willing to embrace it.

When Bill Douglas and Drew Hall first shared their manuscript with me, I immediately recognized the pattern of industry transformation. Having built and scaled Vungle from a startup to a global enterprise with hundreds of employees across eight international offices, I've seen firsthand how proper technology implementation creates exponential value. *Peak Property Performance* isn't just another real estate book—it's a comprehensive framework for transforming certain cost centers into profit engines through the strategic uses of data and digital infrastructure.

The authors' 5C Framework—Clarify, Connect, Collect, Coordinate, and Control—provides the structure needed to navigate this transformation. Throughout my entrepreneurial journey, I've learned that scaling isn't just about growing bigger—it's about growing smarter. The mindset shifts outlined in this book are exactly what commercial real estate leaders need to make the leap from traditional thinking to data-driven excellence.

What resonates most strongly for me is the authors' emphasis on culture and vision. When scaling my companies, I discovered that culture isn't what you say—it's what you do. Every decision you make sends signals to your organization about what matters. Douglas and Hall clearly understand this dynamic, offering practical guidance on how property owners can build organizations that leverage data while maintaining alignment with core values.

The sports analogies throughout the book make complex technological concepts accessible and engaging. Just as championship teams combine individual talent with systematic execution, top-performing properties require both cutting-edge systems and the organizational discipline to leverage them effectively. For those who've been playing "checkers" while the competition advances to "chess," this book provides the strategic upgrade needed to compete at the highest level.

One of the book's greatest strengths is how Douglas and Hall distill their decades of industry experience into a compelling narrative through the fictional Victors Real Estate (VRE) Group. This storytelling approach lets readers experience firsthand how a typical real estate company can transform its operations through data ownership and digital infrastructure. While VRE is fictional, every challenge they face and solution they implement comes directly from the authors' extensive work with actual clients. This approach makes complex concepts immediately accessible and demonstrates how strategies that have revolutionized other industries can be applied practically in commercial real estate.

What separates *Peak Property Performance* from theoretical works is its practicality. The authors don't just theorize about potential—they provide detailed implementation strategies, real-world examples, and actionable tools that readers can apply immediately. The Data & Digital Infrastructure Audit alone can transform your NOI by revealing opportunities in your existing systems. Most properties have networks, video surveillance, internet services, and control systems provided by contractors motivated by their own interests.

The commercial real estate industry stands at an inflection point. Portfolios with suboptimal performance suffer from higher operating expenses, lower net operating incomes, and unfavorable metrics that matter to lenders and investors. The authors demonstrate how their 5C framework addresses all your cost centers and pays special attention to the big three: utilities, vacancies, and insurance.

The winners of tomorrow won't just be those with the best locations or the most capital. They'll be the people who harness the power of their data to drive unprecedented operational efficiencies and create new revenue streams. This parallels my experience in advertising technology, where the ability to leverage data ultimately determined which companies thrived and which disappeared.

Whether you're managing a single property or overseeing a vast portfolio, this book offers the roadmap to transform your real estate operation from average to exceptional. In a world where nearly every industry has been revolutionized by technology, commercial real estate can no longer afford to stand still.

Every commercial real estate professional needs this book. *Peak Property Performance* breaks down the critical elements of digital transformation and shows how to leverage AI and data for unmatched operational efficiency and profitability. Douglas and Hall have created an essential guide for anyone determined to build a championship-level real estate operation in the digital age.

—Zain Jaffer
Partner, Blue Field Capital
Owner, Zain Ventures Family Office
Co-Founder, Vungle

Hail to the Victors?

"To be successful at anything, the truth is you don't have to be special. You just have to be what most people aren't: consistent, determined, and willing to work for it. No shortcuts."

—Tom Brady, NFL quarterback and seven-time Super Bowl champion (including five Super Bowl MVPs)

LOOKING BEYOND AVERAGE

Vance and Vicki, the dynamic duo behind Victors Real Estate Group (VRE), are the epitome of hard work paying off—to a point. As former college athletes, they've carried their competitive spirit into the world of **commercial real estate (CRE)**, amassing an impressive and diverse portfolio of properties across the country. From office buildings to apartments, from student housing to hotels, they've built what many would consider a successful empire. Their investors are happy, their properties are occupied, and they're turning a profit. By all conventional metrics, they're winning the game.

But beneath the surface of their apparent success lies a world of untapped potential. Vance and Vicki run their business the way "everyone else" does it, never questioning the status quo. They signed bulk agreements with **internet service providers (ISPs)**, giving away 90 percent of significant recurring tech services revenue for the sake of convenience. Their building systems—from video surveillance to climate controls—are a patchwork of standalone networks, each operating in isolation and draining resources. Even when they invest in "smart" technology, like advanced lighting or smart locks and thermostats, the systems sit dormant or underutilized for years, their potential locked away in closets full of blinking lights that no one understands.

VRE's property managers focus solely on filling vacancies and minimizing complaints while their building engineers scramble reactively from one problem to the next. Vance and Vicki have no real grasp on the wealth of data their properties are generating or the value that lies within it. They can't tell you how many people use their facilities on a given day or which areas of their buildings are underutilized. They're flying blind, relying on gut feelings and outdated practices instead of on complex data, integrated **digital infrastructures**, and strategic insights.

In essence, Vance and Vicki are leaving money (and many other benefits) on the table. They're not dumb; they're just average and busy in a world where average is increasingly insufficient.

As the CRE industry begins to wake up to the power of data, digital infrastructure, and **artificial intelligence (AI)**, Vance and Vicki stand at a crossroads.[1] Will they continue down the path of mediocrity? Or

---

1   The Massachusetts Institute of Technology defines artificial intelligence as "the technology used to imitate human intelligence, enabling machines to learn and perform tasks typically associated with human intellect." See, Massachusetts Institute of Technology, "Artificial Intelligence vs Machine Learning: What's the Difference?" MIT Professional Education, n.d., https://professionalprograms.mit.edu/blog/technology/machine-learning-vs-artificial-intelligence.

will they seize the opportunity to transform their business and build a true real estate dynasty? The potential is there, hidden in plain sight, just waiting for them to see the playing field more clearly—and take action.

NO INDUSTRY LEFT BEHIND . . .
EXCEPT COMMERCIAL REAL ESTATE?

Vance and Vicki may be hypothetical, but their approach mirrors that of many real-world CRE operators, including clients of OpticWise, a company that specializes in creating intelligent and highly profitable buildings through data and digital infrastructure ownership, and others. We—Bill Douglas and Drew Hall, the authors of this book—are the leadership and founders behind OpticWise, which is at the forefront of transforming the commercial real estate industry's approach to data and digital. After seeing these struggles, these strategies, and these successes time and time again, we decided to share them in this book, through these two hypothetical lead characters.

At OpticWise, our mission is to guide real estate groups like VRE from industry standard to dynasty status, by harnessing the power of data and digital ownership. As our CEO, Bill brings over three decades of entrepreneurial experience and a track record of leading companies onto the Inc. 5000 list. His innovative approaches enable property owners to create wholly owned digital ecosystems that drive income growth and improve operational efficiency. And Drew, our founder and chief systems architect, leverages his expertise in designing high-performance networks to develop solutions that empower owners to unlock the full potential of their data and digital infrastructure assets. Throughout this book, we'll cite examples from our professional experience, walking you through this transformation, demonstrating how owning and leveraging your data and digital infrastructure can revolutionize your operations, boost profitability, and position you as a leader in the evolving commercial real estate landscape.

Simply put, this book is about two questions:

(1) Who owns and controls your data?

(2) Who owns and operates your digital infrastructure?

. . . and one big idea:

**Imagine what you could do if you had
full control of these two things.**

Because with full control of your data and your digital infrastructure, you could apply AI to transform CRE operations as you know it, resulting in the magic formula:

**Data ownership + digital infrastructure ownership +
AI = actionable intelligence**

VRE's approach to its properties is far from the data-driven strategies some other industries employ. While Vance and Vicki struggle to see beyond traditional metrics, these other industries have long recognized the immense value of data and digital infrastructure ownership and AI-driven insights. A 2024 *Chicago Booth Review* article highlighted that "AI is transforming practically every sector of the economy . . . In finance, LLMs [large language models] are mining public data to find varied and largely unexploited investment opportunities—and are evolving from being analytical tools to capable decision-makers, paired with investors in the ongoing hunt for profit."[2]

Let's look at how three large, very different industry sectors—e-commerce logistics, automotive manufacturing, and finance—leverage data and digital technologies to drive efficiency, safety, and profitability. These examples highlight the stark contrast between commercial real estate's common but outdated approach and the data-driven strategies that are reshaping industries and creating market leaders.

Example #1: Retail Distribution Center

Modern distribution centers are marvels of data-driven efficiency. Every aspect of their operations is monitored, analyzed, and optimized in real time. They also own the neural pathways through which this data flows inside their facility. AI algorithms predict product demand, allowing for strategic inventory placement across their network. Robotic systems, guided by machine learning, efficiently pick and pack orders. The movement of workers, the flow of goods, and even the routes of delivery trucks are all tracked and continuously optimized. And the retailer owns all this data, from the moment an item enters its inventory facility to when it reaches the customer's doorstep.

This analytical approach also applies to every piece of operating equipment deployed. This comprehensive data ownership allows

---

2   Monika Brown, "What AI Sees in the Market (That You Might Not)," *Chicago Booth Review*, September 3, 2024, https://www.chicagobooth.edu/review/what-ai-sees-market-that-you-might-not.

retailers to make rapid, informed decisions; reduce costs; and provide the lightning-fast delivery times that have become their hallmark.

Example #2: Automotive Assembly Plant

At an automotive company's final assembly plant, data and AI form the backbone of the entire operation. Every step of the assembly process is meticulously tracked and analyzed. AI-powered quality control systems use computer vision to detect defects the human eye might miss. Predictive maintenance algorithms anticipate when machinery needs servicing, preventing costly breakdowns. The plant's digital infrastructure, which is wholly owned by the manufacturer, enables data aggregation from real-time monitoring of every aspect of production. This includes tracking the location and status of each vehicle as it moves through the assembly line, monitoring the performance of robotic systems, and even analyzing the movements of human workers to optimize ergonomics and efficiency.

By owning and leveraging this data, the manufacturer and its parent company can continually refine processes, improve quality, and respond quickly to any issues, maintaining their edge in the competitive automotive industry.

Example #3: Leading Financial Institutions

While much is publicly known about data and digital infrastructure within companies like Amazon and Ford, leading financial institutions are notoriously protective of their technological capabilities, treating them as closely guarded trade secrets. But we do know that these firms work aggressively to build and maintain proprietary trading platforms, data aggregation systems, and analytical tools that give them competitive advantages in global markets. Top investment banks spend billions building their own computer systems and networks that can instantly analyze everything from standard market information (like stock prices and how many shares are being traded) to newer types of data (like social media trends or satellite images of retail parking lots).

Furthermore, many leading firms have spent hundreds of millions of dollars to move their data centers physically closer to the trading floors to save milliseconds on data transmission. While the specific implementations remain confidential, we know these firms are constantly advancing their AI and machine learning capabilities to enhance trading strategies, improve client service, and manage risk more effectively. This focus on owning and controlling their digital destiny, rather than relying on third-party vendors, allows them to rapidly adapt to changing market conditions and maintain their edge in an industry where microseconds can mean millions of dollars in profit or loss.

ARE YOU A CONTENDER OR A CHAMPION?

As you can see, industries from e-commerce to investment to manufacturing (as well as most others not discussed here) leverage data and digital infrastructure and AI to build sustainable, dominant market positions. These companies are like the great sports dynasties that consistently outperform their rivals year after year. Now ask yourself: Do you want to be like the six-time world champion Chicago Bulls basketball team of the 1990s or like the Cleveland Browns, the perennial bottom-feeders of the National Football League for most of their existence?

With this in mind, real estate owners, operators, managers, and investors are in a position to start asking big questions about where they want to be as this technological revolution takes shape. If Victors Real Estate Group represents the average, many in the industry are still competing like a middling team, content with playing the game but never genuinely contending for a championship or becoming a dynasty.

What are these average performers missing? Why are so many people in commercial real estate interested in remaining on the bench while other industries are changing the game?

In our industry, there's a pervasive *If it ain't broke, don't fix it* mentality. Many, like VRE, stick to traditional metrics of occupancy rates and basic financial returns. They are content with the income being generated already. They don't want to make the change or do the work.

We get it. Everyone has a fear of the unknown, the upfront costs, or even the uncertainty around **return on investment (ROI)**. In our role as CRE technology entrepreneurs, we've heard everything. Owners and management often start saying things like, "I could never afford to do something like that," "Is it really worth it?" and "What's my return?" And let's not forget: "We're not a tech company; we just lease up buildings."

What's at stake here goes far beyond immediate costs or short-term returns. Just as a sports team risks falling behind if they fail to adapt to new training methods or tactical innovations, real estate groups that ignore the power of data and AI risk becoming increasingly irrelevant in a rapidly evolving market. They're leaving money on the table, just like Vance and Vicki did—not just in terms of immediate cost savings or revenue opportunities, but also in their ability to provide better services; attract and retain tenants; and create more valuable, efficient, and sustainable properties.

GOOD SPORTS: Serving Up Gold[3]

To illustrate how innovation can lead to market dominance, let's look at a recent example from the world of sports.

In beach volleyball, the Swedish duo of David Åhman and Jonatan Hellvig perfected an innovative technique called the "Swedish Jump-Set." This move involves a player jumping as if to spike the ball, but instead setting it to their partner. The misdirection forces opponents to commit to blocking a spike that never comes, leaving them out of position for the actual attack. While Polish players initially pioneered this technique, the Swedes refined it from a young age, making it a cornerstone of their strategy. Their commitment to this unconventional approach propelled them to the top of the world rankings and ultimately to Olympic gold in Paris at the age of twenty-two!

In the world of commercial real estate, we must adopt a similar mindset of innovation and refinement. Just as the Swedish Jump-Set combines existing elements (jumping and setting) in a novel way to create a competitive advantage, we must blend our industry knowledge with cutting-edge data analytics and AI to revolutionize our operations. This could mean using predictive analytics to anticipate market trends, employing AI to optimize building systems, or leveraging big data to uncover new revenue streams. By fully committing to these technologies and continuously refining our approach, we can create our own "Jump-Set" moment—a game-changing strategy that leaves competitors scrambling to adapt.

In doing so, we won't just be participating in the market; we'll be shaping its future, winning gold medals in our field by consistently staying one jump ahead of the competition.

---

3   Jimmy Golen, "Jump-setting Swedes Beat Germany to Win the Olympic Beach Volleyball Gold Medal," Associated Press, August 10, 2024, https://apnews.com/article/2024-olympics-beach-volleyball-men-0da8308fd2ff-8c1f11549d86bd27d1d4; Jimmy Golen, "'Swedish Jump-Set' Helps World's Top Beach Volleyball Team Reach the Medal Round at Paris Olympics," Associated Press, August 7, 2024, https://apnews.com/article/2024-olympics-sweden-jumpset-8157af02d1be448777d9201bc09efcbb.

continued

Key Takeaways for Real Estate

Like the two young men who perfected the revolutionary Swedish Jump-Set technique, successful real estate operators need to:

- Innovate by combining existing elements in new ways.
- Commit fully to refining and perfecting your approach.
- Use misdirection to stay ahead of competitors.
- Turn unconventional strategies into cornerstones of your success.

The choice facing CRE organizations isn't whether to innovate but how quickly one can catch up to the front-runners. The question is, will groups like VRE continue to play like a midlevel team, or will they seize the opportunity to build a true dynasty, leveraging data and AI to maximize their **net operating income (NOI)** and dominate their market for years to come?

We're here to reassure you: Becoming a champion in commercial real estate is within your reach. By developing the right vision, assembling a strong team, implementing smart strategies, employing effective tactics, and fostering a collaborative culture, you can achieve business outcomes beyond the boundaries of your imagination today.

For now, we invite you to take a courtside seat with us. We'll guide you through the process of entering the game and ultimately lead you to success. Pick your favorite sport as an analogy—we'll get you to the winner's circle, the victor's podium, the trophy presentation, or that victory lap you deserve.

But before we dive into the action, let's clarify the crucial benefits of owning your data, controlling your digital infrastructure, and leveraging AI for you and your team. These elements form the foundation of modern commercial real estate success. Understanding their importance is the first step toward transforming your business.

ONLY BENEFITS

When real estate owners like Vance and Vicki take control of their digital destiny, the benefits are far-reaching and transformative. By owning their data and digital infrastructure and harnessing the power of AI, they can unlock a new realm of possibilities that extend far beyond traditional real estate metrics.

This book uses Vance, Vicki, and Victors Real Estate Group—and loads of sports examples—as models to show you a step-by-step approach to creating tremendous benefits for your business and your portfolio. The book's many sports analogies illuminate the path to peak property performance. Just as championship teams require the right combination of talent, strategy, and execution, building a real estate dynasty demands excellence across multiple domains.

To help you navigate these parallels, we've mapped out key elements of sports success alongside their CRE counterparts (see Figure 1). This framework will serve as your reference point as we explore how to transform your properties from average performers into market champions.

Figure 1. Sports vs. Commercial Real Estate

Sports	CRE
Arena	CRE Vertical
Ownership	Ownership
Management/general manager (GM)	Management
Coaches	Asset and property managers
Trainers	Building engineers

continued

Athlete/team performance	Property/site performance
Playbook	AI strategy
Fans/experience	Tenants/user experience (UX)
Team stats/*Moneyball*	Data source/data lake
Revenues	Revenues
Operating expenses	Operating expenses
↑↓ Profits	↑↓ NOI

Just as a sports dynasty leverages every aspect of the game—from player statistics to advanced analytics—to maintain its competitive edge, forward-thinking real estate groups harness the power of data, digital infrastructure, and AI to create sustainable success. While we are often quick to focus on the financial benefits of this process, other critical, purpose- and values-driven benefits can also give your organization and properties that championship edge (see Figure 2).

Financial Benefits

By taking control of their digital infrastructure and data, CRE owners can unlock significant financial benefits. For instance, instead of settling for a mere 4 percent revenue share from bulk internet agreements, owners should earn up to $400 per door annually. **Smart building** systems, when properly utilized, can lead to substantial operational savings to further increase NOI. Imagine the impact of a smart lighting system that's actually connected and optimized rather than sitting dormant in a closet. Systems like these can reduce energy costs while simultaneously increasing the property's value through improved efficiencies and increased tenant retention.

Figure 2. Peak-Performing Vision: The Benefits of Owning Data and Digital Infrastructure and Using AI

Domain	Benefits
Financial	• Increased revenue from additional services and optimized space utilization • Reduced energy costs through smart systems optimization • Lower maintenance costs via identifying predictive maintenance opportunities • Reduced expenses from utilities and insurance • New revenue streams from data and technology monetization • Improved asset valuation due to increased NOI
Operational	• Shift from reactive to proactive management • Improved tenant satisfaction and retention • Enhanced employee productivity and job satisfaction • Better safety through intelligent monitoring • Improved sustainability • Optimized space utilization • Streamlined vendor management
Competitive	• Market differentiation through smart, connected spaces • Ability to command premium rents • Attraction and retention of high-value tenants • Improved investor appeal • Industry leadership position • Future-proofing against technological disruption • Data-driven continuous improvement and innovation

Operational Benefits

The operational advantages of a data-driven approach are equally compelling. With the right sensors and analytics, operations managers can shift from reactive to proactive maintenance. Instead of waiting for a tenant to report a leak—a delay that can cause potentially thousands of dollars in damage—owners who have installed sensors can detect issues early, preventing costly repairs and disruptions. This proactive stance extends to all aspects of building management—everything from **heating, ventilation, and air-conditioning (HVAC)** systems to elevator maintenance.

Imagine being able to optimize common area temperatures based on real-time and planned occupancy data, or adjusting cleaning schedules to match foot traffic patterns. As one property manager noted, knowing how many people are in the building on any given day could help optimize energy use and improve tenant services, along with reducing expenses.

Furthermore, for employees, having access to comprehensive building data means less stress and more efficient problem-solving. Companies that use this playbook generally have a more engaged and happier workforce.

Competitive Advantages

Perhaps the most compelling reason to embrace data ownership and AI is the competitive advantage it provides. In a market where most players are content with average performance, those who leverage these technologies can create a significant competitive edge. By offering unique services to tenants, optimizing their operations in ways competitors can't match, and making more informed investment decisions, they consistently one-up the other contenders.

This advantage extends to attracting and retaining top stakeholders. In a world where companies are increasingly data-driven, tenants, banks, insurers, municipalities, contractors, and others prefer properties that can provide them with insights and efficiencies that others can't. Whether it's detailed occupancy analytics or energy usage data for environmentally conscious tenants, these capabilities can set a property apart in a crowded market.

Just as sports dynasties use every tool at their disposal to stay ahead of the competition, savvy real estate owners are using these technological advantages to build sustainable, long-term success in an increasingly competitive market. By embracing data ownership, investing in robust digital infrastructure, and leveraging AI, real estate groups can transform from average players into market leaders. You can create a virtuous cycle of improved operations, innovative solutions, increased tenant satisfaction, and enhanced profitability.

But you have to be willing to take the leap.

JUST DO IT!

It's time to stop playing in the minor leagues and start building your dynasty. This book is your guide for transforming from an average player into a real estate champion. We're not here to pat you on the back for your current success; we're here to show you how much more you could achieve if you "just do it"!

Before we enter the arena, be sure to note the following two major concepts in your guide.

1. **Data ownership + digital infrastructure ownership + AI = actionable intelligence.** This formula is your secret weapon. It's not just about collecting data; it's about owning that data, along with all of your networks, and turning it into insights you can act on. Remember that so-called smart system that's been sitting dormant for years in the closet? That's the difference between having equipment and having intelligence.

2. **Tech transformation is a team sport.** Just like you can't win a championship with a team composed of a single star player, you

can't transform your real estate business with just one tech guru. From the property managers to the CFO, everyone needs to be on board. It's about aligning your entire team on the benefits we've talked about: financial gains, operational efficiencies, and competitive advantages.

Now, let's break down our game plan into five strategic moves—the five *C*'s in the 5C Framework, each of which is explored in the next five chapters. Think of these as the key plays that will take you from being like Victors Real Estate to being the real estate victors!

The 5C Framework

 **CLARIFY** (CHAPTER 1)

We're going to help you see your properties through a new lens. You will gather information about your properties, systems, **hardware**, teams, and so forth. We'll ensure you assess and thereby know every digital asset, data source, and operational opportunity in your portfolio.

 **CONNECT** (CHAPTER 2)

No more isolated systems! We'll show you how to connect everything—from that standalone video surveillance to your smart thermostats. Creating a unified digital nervous system for your properties will help you ensure peak performance.

COLLECT (CHAPTER 3)

This is where we bring together your all-star lineup of people, systems, data, and infrastructure. We're not just talking about hiring data help; we're talking about creating a data-driven culture across your entire organization, starting from the top. We'll help you focus on collecting all of your data in a single location that you own and control.

COORDINATE (CHAPTER 4)

Time for training camp, where we transform individual talents into a championship team. We'll get all of your systems playing the same game, running from the unified playbook, and communicating seamlessly. Imagine your building anticipating its own needs, making real-time adjustments like a quarterback reads the defense. You'll have the insight of a coach up in the booth, spotting opportunities and potential issues before they happen.

CONTROL (CHAPTER 5)

Start calling the shots based on real-time, actionable intelligence. We'll help you set up dashboards that give you a bird's-eye view of your entire portfolio, identify the initiatives that promise the most significant impact, and get your entire management team thinking like data-driven champions.

Once you reach this fifth level, executives and owners may choose to achieve another final *C*: You may become a champion, as discussed in the final chapter.

 CHAMPION (CHAPTER 6)

With your systems and initial successes in place, it's time to transform yourself and your organization for sustainable excellence. Like great sports dynasties, peak performance requires more than just good systems—it demands visionary leadership and organizational transformation. We'll show you how to make the crucial transition from working *in* your business to working *on* it, building your talent pipeline and creating a culture of excellence. You'll learn to move from the field to the skybox, seeing your entire portfolio with strategic clarity while applying data-driven insights at scale.

At this point, the focus shifts from individual property success to portfolio-wide excellence, requiring new levels of personal stamina and strategic thinking. Through this evolution in leadership and systematic optimization, you won't just be managing properties—you'll be building a commercial real estate dynasty that stands the test of time.

Like the gold medalist Swedish beach volleyball duo, we need to perfect our own jump-set in real estate—a unique combination of data ownership, digital infrastructure, and AI that will leave our competitors scrambling to adapt. In the following chapters, we'll dive deep into each of these strategies, showing you exactly how to implement them in your business. We'll share real-world examples, provide practical tools, and guide you step-by-step toward becoming a data-driven, AI-enabled CRE powerhouse.

Remember Vance and Vicki? Like them, you're intelligent and hard-working. But we've collaborated with enough clients to know we can all work smarter. Why settle for average in a world where average isn't good enough? It's time to stop leaving all those benefits and money on the table and start building a real estate dynasty.

Are you ready to just do it?

CHAPTER 1

Clarify: Entering the Arena

"I believe in the basics: attention to, and perfection of,
tiny details that might be commonly overlooked. . . .
They are the difference between champions
and near champions."

—John Wooden, legendary UCLA basketball coach
and ten-time NCAA champion

GAME ON!

Vance and Vicki, the founders and leaders of Victors Real Estate Group (VRE), sat in their sleek downtown office, surrounded by blueprints and financial reports. Despite their apparent success, a recent meeting with their bank had left them uneasy. The banker's words still rang in their ears. "Your ratios are off," he'd said. "These market changes are bringing you close to being out of covenant."

The couple had exchanged worried glances. Their returns—consistent yet average—might not be enough for Victors Real Estate Group to thrive in today's market.

At the root of their problem was the changing economic land-scape: The steady climb of interest rates had put pressure on their debt-to-income ratios. Their once-comfortable margins were now being squeezed by rising **operating expenses (OpEx)**, particularly in utilities, insurance, and maintenance. To make matters worse, occupancy rates in some of their older properties started slipping as newer, more technologically advanced buildings entered the market. The bank, sensing increased risk, was now demanding improved returns in order to maintain VRE's loans.

Vance and Vicki realized they were facing a critical juncture: innovate and improve their portfolio's performance or risk being forced to sell off assets.

Determined not to let their real estate portfolio fall apart, they needed a fresh perspective. Their current operations strategies, while solid by traditional standards, clearly were no longer enough. They needed new advice and direction from someone who could help them see beyond the conventional metrics of occupancy rates and rental income—someone who could unlock the hidden potential in their properties and bring them into the digital age.

Vicki suddenly remembered a conversation they'd had at a recent real estate conference about the transformative power of **data and digital infrastructure** in property operations. Perhaps it was time, she and Vance decided, to bring in some experts.

Eager to stay ahead, they called in a pair of CRE technology consultants, Dave and Kaylie from OpticWise, to discuss how they could build truly championship properties. As the consultants entered the conference room, Vance leaned forward, his competitive spirit from his college athlete days kicking in. "We've got properties across the country," he began, "but we need to do better. How can we turn these average-performing properties into champions?"

Dave, a seasoned executive and consultant, smiled knowingly. "First things first," he said, pulling out a tablet. "We need to see your properties with new eyes. We'll start by identifying every digital asset, every data source, and every opportunity on a couple of your properties. Let's begin with the properties where you think we can make an impact."

Vicki raised an eyebrow, intrigued. "What do you mean by 'every data source'?" she asked. "We've got our financial reports right here."

Kaylie, a true digital architect, was no stranger to consulting with hesitant clients. "Those reports are just the tip of the iceberg," she explained, nodding her head. "We're talking about auditing *all* of your systems—physical and digital, from your HVAC and security systems to your internet infrastructure and beyond. It's time to uncover the hidden potential in your properties."

Both Vance and Vicki perked up at those words, feeling a strong uptick in energy. They were about to see their properties in a whole new light, with Dave and Kaylie as their guide. The goal? To gain clarity on their digital infrastructure and the data assets that can impact both their residents' experience and VRE's bottom line.

Chapter 1 Goals

In this chapter, we tackle Clarity—the first critical step in building a championship real estate portfolio. Just as winning teams must thoroughly understand their roster's true capabilities before they can compete at the highest level, you'll learn to see your properties' full technological potential.

We'll show you how to use the **Data & Digital Infrastructure**

continued

Audit (DDIA) tool to uncover hidden value, navigate the six key areas of digital infrastructure that exist in every building, and apply five game-changing questions to evaluate and maximize your technology investments.

Whether you're working with existing buildings or planning new construction, you'll gain the tools required to see beyond traditional metrics and transform average properties into real estate champions. Are you ready to step into the arena and build your dynasty?

FROM CLOUDY TO CLARITY

Clarifying your digital infrastructure—and the data it generates—involves thoroughly checking all physical and digital systems within your property. This process goes beyond identifying traditional assets like HVAC and security systems; it also encompasses newer technologies such as **Internet of Things (IoT)** devices, smart systems, advanced energy management systems, and so forth. The goal is to create a clear picture of your entire technology ecosystem.

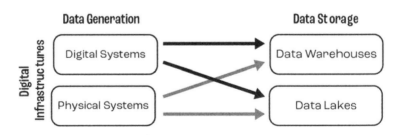

Digital infrastructures are composed of the following elements:

- **Digital systems** include the multiple CRE software-driven platforms employed to operate a property. These systems, which process and may even store their own generated data, include HVAC, the **building management systems (BMS)**, the **building automation systems (BAS)**, leak detection, security and parking systems, and many others.
- **Physical systems** are the various hardware and tangible apparatus, including the equipment and networks that form the backbone of a CRE facility. Physical systems comprise wires, sensors, networks, switches, racks, cabinets, displays, computers (desktops, notebooks, servers), and such.

Data infrastructures, on the other hand, comprise the following:

- **Data warehouses and data lakes** store the digital data created by all the systems listed earlier. (See appendix D for more on the distinction between lakes and warehouses.)
- **Data pools** are created by individual digital or physical systems within any property.

Start by gaining an understanding of what systems you have, how they're physically and digitally connected, what data they're generating, and who owns that data and infrastructure. This requires examining everything from the cables running through your walls to the cloud-based software managing your various operations.

For instance, you might discover that your property has occupancy sensors installed but they are not being properly utilized, or that your access control system is generating valuable foot traffic data that you're not leveraging. You might find that your energy management system is capable of much more granular control than you currently employ or that your tenant management software contains a wealth of untapped insights about lease patterns and tenant preferences.

Notably, citing a real estate technology survey conducted in 2023, Jones Lang LaSalle reported that "most companies are struggling to realize the benefits of the technologies they've already adopted; fewer than 40 percent consider their existing tech programs to be very successful in meeting their initial objectives."[4] One Top 50 Operator according to the National Multifamily Housing Council illustrated this challenge in a survey conducted by OpticWise with Enoch & Company, providing a ground-level perspective by sharing how "innovations tend to be fragmented"—such as "separate apps for different functions that become obsolete," and "door lock systems where the first to market is [now] out of business."[5]

To move beyond these muddled approaches to data and digital infrastructures, you and your team need to work toward clarity and a shared vision. Why does clarity matter so much? Because with an honest, well-defined evaluation of your current data and digital infrastructures, you can achieve a number of crucial, transformative goals for your CRE organization, including the following.

---

4   Jones Lang LaSalle, Inc., *Global Real Estate Technology Survey*, October 2023, https://www.jllt.com/research/global-real-estate-technology-survey-2023.

5   Enoch & Company, *What Owners Want: Insights for Future-Ready Living—2024 Edition*, https://doc.opticwise.cloud/future-ready-living.

Identify Inefficiencies and Redundancies

Many property owners unknowingly pay for multiple networks or systems that could be consolidated instead. Why tolerate multiple, disparate networks within a building when one unified system would be more efficient, cost-effective, resilient, and powerful? For example, you might needlessly be maintaining separate networks for security cameras, HVAC controls, and internet access, each with its own **capital expenditures (CapEx)**, maintenance costs, and complexities. By identifying redundancies, you can potentially save tens of thousands of dollars annually per property.

Uncover Hidden Asset Value

Many buildings have underutilized or dormant smart systems. By auditing all of your systems, you might discover powerful tools for energy optimization, predictive maintenance, and improved tenant satisfaction that you're not fully leveraging. Activating these systems could significantly increase your property's efficiency and value.

Maintain Data Ownership and Control

In today's digital age, many property owners inadvertently give away valuable data to vendors. For instance, your elevator maintenance company might collect usage data that could inform your energy management strategies, or your parking system might gather information about visitor patterns that could optimize your retail mix. By clarifying data ownership, you can take control of these valuable data assets, drive better decision-making, reduce operating expenses, and create new revenue streams.

Assess How Well Systems Work

The process of assessing your existing infrastructure can reveal opportunities for improvement or replacement of underperforming systems. By ensuring every piece of your digital infrastructure contributes to your property's success, you can maximize overall performance and value.

Trust the Process

Gaining clarity on the physical and digital systems within your digital infrastructure requires a systematic process. It takes time, effort, expertise, and a deeply methodical approach to unearth all the information you need to get your properties operating at the championship level. This process typically involves the following steps:

1. Physical inspection. Schedule a thorough walkthrough of your properties, identifying and documenting all visible technology assets. Your staff is fully capable of this, given the proper direction. In fact, they may have done this already, but we often find that little to no network documentation has been completed.

2. Documentation review. Examine all available system documentation, including user manuals, network diagrams, and maintenance records.

3. Stakeholder interviews. Speak with staff and vendors (and sometimes even tenants) to understand how systems are being used and what pain points exist.

4. Data sources and storage analysis. Review the outputs of your various systems to understand what data is being generated, how it is (or isn't) being used, where it is stored, and who owns it.

5. Contract and ownership review. Examine all technology-related contracts to understand terms, ownership clauses, and service levels. The bottom line is, who owns and controls what?

6. Gap analysis. Identify discrepancies between what systems you have, what you're actually using, and what you need.

7. Recommendation development. Based on all the aforementioned steps, create a plan for optimizing your digital infrastructure and gathering all of your disparate data.

This assessment process can be challenging, especially for larger or older portfolios. You may encounter resistance from staff who are comfortable with existing systems or vendors who benefit from the status quo. You might also face technical challenges when connecting to legacy systems or extracting data from proprietary platforms. Stand firm and resolve to move forward with your long-term goals in mind. The potential benefits of gaining clarity around your digital infrastructure far outweigh these temporary hurdles.

WHAT'S IN YOUR CLUBHOUSE? THE SIX KEY AREAS OF DIGITAL INFRASTRUCTURE

As we dive deeper into the world of CRE data and digital infrastructures, it's crucial to understand the various systems and data types that exist within a property. These systems, when properly optimized, can transform a building from a static asset into a dynamic, responsive environment that enhances tenant experience, reduces costs, and unlocks new income streams.

As Dave and Kaylie emphasized in their consultation with Vance and Vicki, many property owners are unaware of the full capabilities of the systems they already have in place. Often they're paying for multiple networks or systems that could be consolidated, or leaving valuable digital assets dormant in those closets full of mysterious blinking lights.

When you begin looking closer at your properties, you will encounter six categories of data and digital infrastructures that you'll need to assess carefully. Let's briefly explore each of these **data and digital infrastructure domains** and how they can be leveraged to create a truly intelligent, efficient, enjoyable, and profitable property.

1. Network Infrastructure and IoT

This foundational category includes systems like common area and tenant WiFi, internet circuits, and voice services. It also encompasses IoT devices such as smart building technologies, leak detection, occupancy sensors, temperature and humidity sensors, and asset tracking systems. These and many other sensors and systems form the backbone of a smart building, enabling communication between various platforms and collecting vital data on building usage and conditions.

Essential role: Supports your entire smart building ecosystem.

2. Security, Access Control, and Risk Management

This category covers traditional security measures like access controls, surveillance, and video recording, as well as broader risk management tools such as insurance or environmental compliance management. These systems not only protect the property but also generate valuable data on building access patterns and potential risks.

Essential role: Protects your assets, your data, and your tenants.

3. Energy, Environmental Management, and Sustainability

This expansive category includes systems for managing energy, water, and air quality. It covers everything from HVAC optimization and smart thermostats to carbon footprint tracking and green building certification management. These systems can significantly reduce OpEx while improving tenant comfort and meeting sustainability goals.

Essential role: Optimizes energy use and reduces costs.

4. Property Operations and Tenant Experience

This category focuses on the day-to-day operations of the property and the enhancement of tenant satisfaction. It includes systems for facilities operations, parking management, and tenant communication platforms. These tools can make operations smoother, improve tenant engagement, and provide valuable insights into how the building is being used.

Essential role: Enhances tenant satisfaction and retention.

5. Financial and Asset Management

This category includes tools for tracking operating expenses, predicting maintenance needs, valuing assets, and analyzing investment performance. These systems provide the insights necessary for making informed decisions about financial and investment strategies.

Essential role: Maximizes returns on your investments.

6. Data Aggregation and Analytics

This forward-looking category encompasses advanced tools for data analysis and predictive modeling. It includes **business intelligence (BI)** platforms, which comprise AI as well as natural language processing (which enables computers to understand, process, and respond to human language), machine learning (which allows AI systems to improve their performance and learn from their experiences), and robotics process automation (the technology that automates manual and repetitive tasks). Also included in this domain are benchmarking tools and predictive analytics that can gather important insights from the wealth of data generated by other systems.

Essential role: Turns raw data into actionable intelligence.

LET'S DO AN AUDIT

As teams gain clarity on these systems and the data they generate, property owners can move beyond focusing solely on traditional metrics like occupancy and rent rolls and start seeing their properties with fresh perspective. Taking this comprehensive viewpoint, owners can identify operational inefficiencies, discover underutilized assets, and develop innovative solutions to set their properties apart in a competitive market.

Notably, one of the most common findings when we do these data and digital inventory audits is expensive, unnecessary redundancies. Continuing with our sports analogy, let's imagine a team chartering multiple private planes, with each flying a single player to a game, instead of using one jet for the whole team. While this idea sounds absurd in the sports context, it is how many buildings operate. We often find that clients have multiple, disconnected physical and digital systems, each running on its own "network plane" instead of on a unified, resilient, secure digital infrastructure.

Our approach is to consolidate these systems into one unified "team plane," reducing costs and complexity while improving overall performance and data integration. This consolidation not only streamlines operations but also opens up new possibilities for data utilization.

In this digital age, it's crucial to remember an oft-repeated mantra: *If you're not monetizing your data, then someone else probably is.* By understanding and optimizing your digital infrastructure and asserting ownership over your data, you can unlock its full potential instead of leaving money on the table. With this shift in perspective, property owners can transform themselves from average players to real estate champions.

Ultimately, performing an audit is the first step in creating properties that are not just rentable spaces but highly profitable assets. By seeing your properties through this new lens and leveraging the power of connected systems and data, you can achieve a level of performance and value creation that sets you apart in the competitive real estate market.

PURPOSE + POTENTIAL = PEAK PERFORMANCE

Just as Billy Beane revolutionized baseball by looking at player statistics in a new way, we can transform real estate operations by reexamining our physical and digital systems. For property owners to maximize an asset's

GOOD SPORTS: Clarify What You've Got

Seeing your assets through a new lens is a powerful approach that can lead to revolutionary change, whether in life generally, in commercial real estate, or in the world of sports. Michael Lewis's groundbreaking book *Moneyball: The Art of Winning an Unfair Game*, later adapted into a critically acclaimed film starring Brad Pitt, tells the story of how General Manager Billy Beane and the Oakland A's revolutionized baseball by looking at things from a different angle.

At its core, *Moneyball* is about gaining clarity on your assets and understanding their true value, a lesson that also resonates powerfully in the world of commercial real estate. Beane and his team realized that traditional scouting methods, which emphasized easily visible attributes like a player's physique or raw power, were overlooking crucial data that truly correlated with winning games. They focused instead on statistics like on-base percentage and slugging percentage (the number of bases players take divided by the number of times they are at bat), which provide a clearer picture of a player's actual contribution to the team's success.

"We're not selling jeans here," Beane often repeated to his scouts—a powerful reminder not to be overly concerned with a player's appearance and other traditional data points. This approach serves real estate professionals just as well, reminding us to clarify and understand the underlying systems and data that can truly enhance value.

The book presents this new way of seeing players in, for example, the drafting of Mark Teahen, a college player overlooked by other teams because he didn't fit the traditional mold of a power-hitting third baseman. While other teams were fixated on home run totals, the A's looked deeper, recognizing that Teahen's high on-base percentage (.493) and slugging percentage (.624) indicated he was an excellent overall hitter with growth potential.

As Beane famously said, "Power is something that can be acquired. Good hitters develop power. Power hitters don't become good hitters."[6] This insight allowed the A's to see value where others didn't. Savvy real estate professionals do the same thing when they find overlooked opportunities by looking beyond surface-level metrics.

The team's approach to clarifying what they had—and what the organization needed—led to remarkable success, allowing the A's to compete with teams that had much larger payrolls. This method of gaining clarity on the true value of assets spread throughout professional baseball, culminating in historic World Series victories for the Boston Red Sox in 2004 and the Chicago Cubs in 2016—both led by Billy Beane's protégé, Theo Epstein.

In commercial real estate, we must adopt a similar mindset. Just as the A's transformed baseball by seeing the game from a new angle, looking deeper into the available data to understand a player's true value, we can revolutionize commercial real estate by looking beyond a property's surface-level attributes or traditional metrics and recognizing what the property truly has to offer.

As a CRE owner, you must develop clarity around your physical and digital infrastructure and the data assets they generate, understanding how they contribute to your success. This is where the magic happens, as you uncover hidden efficiencies, create new revenue streams, and achieve unprecedented value for tenants, management, and owners alike.

Key Takeaways for Real Estate

- Clarify new, meaningful metrics.
- Challenge traditional valuation methods.
- Identify and leverage undervalued assets.
- Use data to drive decision-making.
- Look beyond surface-level appearances to find true value.

---

6   Michael Lewis, *Moneyball: The Art of Winning an Unfair Game* (W. W. Norton, 2004).

value, we need to understand the purpose, potential, and performance of each data and digital infrastructure domain. The fundamental lessons from *Moneyball* directly apply to the CRE industry: Clarify new and meaningful metrics. Challenge traditional valuation methods. Identify and leverage undervalued assets. Use data to drive decision-making. And look beyond surface-level appearances to find true value.

To apply this approach to real estate, we need to ask the right questions about our assets. As Dave and Kaylie had explained to Vance and Vicki, asking the following five key questions about any tool or asset can uncover hidden potential and drive significant improvements in your properties:

1. What are you trying to accomplish with this digital tool (including software and data)? Property owners need to understand the real purpose of each piece of digital infrastructure and data flow. That's why this question is crucial: It forces property owners to clearly state what they want to achieve with each system.

   For example, consider an intelligent lighting system. Is it merely turning lights on and off, or could it be doing more? A well-utilized lighting system could optimize energy usage, provide valuable occupancy data, or even improve tenant experience through customizable lighting scenarios at certain times of the day. By clearly defining your objectives, you can ensure you're leveraging each tool to its fullest potential.

2. Does this tool meet your requirements? Many systems are capable of much more than their current use. So, this question goes beyond just checking whether the system is functioning. Even a yes answer leaves room for improvement.

Take, for example, a building management system. On the surface, it might appear to be meeting basic requirements for indoor environmental control. However, digging deeper, you might discover advanced features that, when activated and integrated with other sensors, could reduce energy consumption by as much as 18 percent. Such an optimization could lead to significant cost savings—for a large property, hundreds of thousands of dollars annually.

If you discover no requirements related to this tool's capabilities, then consider removing it from the property. There is no need to keep a system forever; just because it's there today doesn't mean it has to be there tomorrow. What's the ROI? If it's low or zero, consider nixing the system.

3. Is each contract aligned with your goals, requirements, and budget? Is the vendor following through, and are its services and terms appropriate? Many vendor contracts escalate over time, and you might be paying for support or services you no longer use. Asking these questions ensures you're getting proper value for the money spent.

    Be wary of contracts that offer attractive initial terms but have steep escalations built in; it's not uncommon for service rates to drastically increase once the initial contract period ends. Regularly review your vendors and contracts for these hidden costs and to ensure you're not overpaying—or paying for obsolete or unused services.

4. Do you own and control the data generated by your physical and digital systems? If the answer is *No, we don't own the data*, then who owns it? If the answer is *yes*, then how can you access

it—or better yet, how can you own and *control* it? This critical question speaks to the heart of data ownership and utilization. Remember, if you're not monetizing your data, then someone else probably is.

Data access can drive significant value in unexpected ways. For instance, data from your access control system could provide insights about space utilization and whether tenants might pay a premium to access that space. Likewise, occupancy data could be used to optimize cleaning schedules or adjust common area temperatures, improving efficiency and reducing costs.

Moreover, understanding your data access is essential for analytics leading to business intelligence. By knowing what data you have access to and how you can access it, you can start to see opportunities for blending data from different systems, unlocking new insights and efficiencies within your portfolio.

5. Do the digital infrastructure and data meet security and privacy standards? Working with vendors, contractors, and consultants who prioritize data security and privacy to protect your new network is critical to the long-term success of any property in the twenty-first century. Furthermore, compliance with data protection regulations is a necessity, as is maintaining transparency with tenants about data collection and usage.

Any data discussed in this book refers specifically to data generated and/or owned by the property and is typically (but not exclusively) focused on operations data. We are advocates for never collecting any user data, and we strongly believe in user privacy. A tenant's data is their data, just as your building's data is your data. Therefore, we strongly recommend *not* collecting any personally identifiable information about tenants—and proudly stating this in your privacy statements. Privacy should be a competitive advantage, positioning the property as not just smart but also secure and respectful of every user's privacy. Why just meet privacy standards when you could *exceed* them?

In essence, these five questions aim to help you see your data and digital infrastructure in new ways. By thoroughly understanding both your data sources and your digital infrastructure—including what they're capable of and who owns each of them—you can find overlooked value and transform your approach to operations and property management. This is how average players in the real estate game become champions, creating properties that are not just spaces but intelligent, efficient, and highly profitable assets.

By systematically applying these questions to each category of data and digital infrastructure, property owners can break free of the status quo, overcome the *If it ain't broke, don't fix it* mentality, and view their properties with renewed insight.

WAIT, WHICH FIELD ARE WE PLAYING ON?

When considering data and digital infrastructure in commercial real estate, it's crucial to understand the distinct opportunities and challenges presented by brownfield (existing property) and greenfield (new construction) projects. These two scenarios have significantly different financial levers and considerations (see Figure 3).

Brownfield projects involve working with existing buildings and infrastructures, often with a focus on expense reduction and improving current setups. Many brownfield properties haven't been thoroughly analyzed in years, leading to unsupported equipment and/or contracts that have transitioned to month-to-month terms with escalating costs.

This situation often presents opportunities for significant cost savings when property owners can reevaluate and renegotiate contracts or improve existing systems that may be underused or improperly configured. Sometimes, antiquated systems should be shut down. And sometimes, upgrades are required to meet new ownership requirements.

Brownfield projects can face challenges, however, particularly in retrofitting. For instance, we've observed that retrofitting apartments with modern WiFi is typically more difficult and expensive than in office buildings. Residential construction has finished surfaces on ceilings, so disruptive and costly renovations are often required to accomplish the retrofit. This can be inconvenient for both the owners and the current tenants.

Despite these complications, the ROI on consolidating and managing the digital infrastructure of brownfield projects, coupled with the benefits of data aggregation, is very attractive, and property owners can expect significant impact on their net operating income (NOI).

Greenfield projects, on the other hand, offer much more flexibility and potential to save on build cost (i.e., CapEx), coupled with long-term additional revenue generation. Designing the digital infrastructure from the ground up can mean fewer networks are needed, potentially reducing the number of data closets and specifying more streamlined, efficient systems.

In greenfield projects, proper planning can significantly reduce both CapEx and OpEx. Avoid the temptation to over-engineer new buildings, incorporating far more cabling and data closets than necessary. This not only wastes valuable, would-be rentable space but also increases build costs unnecessarily.

Figure 3. Greenfield vs. Brownfield: A Comparison

Factor	Impact on Brownfield (Existing Properties)	Impact on Greenfield (New Construction)
CapEx	**Low to Medium** • Limited by system upgrades • Apartment retrofit costs can be significant for some systems	**High** • Opportunity to significantly impact total build cost • Can specify all digital infrastructure
OpEx	**Medium to High** • Potential for significant reduction • May have existing inefficient systems	**Medium to High** • Can design for optimal efficiency • Opportunity to minimize operating costs
Revenue	**Low to Medium** • Limited by existing infrastructure • Potential for some new services • Cost savings driven	**Medium to High** • New revenue streams • Full flexibility in service offerings • Both revenue and savings driven

In summary, brownfield projects should focus on expense reduction and the optimization of existing systems; they tend to involve not only more challenges but also greater costs to achieve new revenue generation. Meanwhile, greenfield projects offer greater flexibility and potential for both long-term OpEx savings and revenue generation; they also present the opportunity for significant CapEx reduction during the build process. By understanding these differences and leveraging the appropriate financial levers, property owners can make informed decisions about optimizing their existing properties and plan effectively. In both cases, however, ownership of data and digital infrastructures is crucial.

We strongly believe that property owners should own their digital infrastructure and everything that attaches to it, *and* should own their data rather than giving that pathway and information away to third parties. In both cases, we aim to move beyond traditional metrics and unlock hidden value. This strategic approach to data and digital infrastructures is key to transforming yourself from an average performer to a real estate champion.

BRING IT ON!

As twilight settled over the city skyline, Vance and Vicki leaned back in their chairs, their minds reeling from the possibilities and questions Dave and Kaylie had presented. The stacks of financial reports that had once seemed so comprehensive now appeared woefully inadequate.

Vance broke the silence, his voice filled with determination. "I think I finally understand what you mean by seeing our properties with new eyes," he said. "We've been so fixated on occupancy rates and pure financials that we've been blind to the untapped potential right under our noses."

Vicki nodded emphatically. "It's like we've been coaching a championship team but only utilizing half our roster, not even realizing the depth of talent we had on the bench."

After a moment of shared reflection, Vance spoke up. "First, I want to tackle our ten-story office building downtown. It's been a solid performer, but with what we've learned today, I bet we could transform it into an MVP."

Vicki's eyes sparkled with excitement. "And that new apartment complex we're planning in the suburbs—we need to completely reimagine our approach. We have an incredible opportunity to build it right from the foundation up, integrating everything we've discussed."

Dave nodded approvingly. "Excellent choices. For the downtown office property, we're looking at potentially boosting your NOI by $0.90 per square foot annually. We'll use a combination of slashing energy costs, creating new revenue streams, leveraging your data, and streamlining operations for peak efficiency."

Kaylie leaned in. "And for the suburban apartment project, we're talking about significant reductions on your initial build costs by optimizing your digital infrastructure design from the get-go. In the long term, you could be looking at up to $650 per door in additional annual NOI generated from new revenues and all the operating savings. That's the power of getting it right from the start."

Vance and Vicki exchanged glances. These projections far exceeded anything they had previously imagined possible.

"So, what's our game plan?" Vicki asked, her voice brimming with enthusiasm. "How do we start transforming these properties from average players into champions?"

"Well, that's where the real work begins," Dave replied. "To unlock the potential of your properties, we need to dive deep into the playbook of data-driven real estate operations. It's not just about installing new systems or collecting data. It's about fundamentally reshaping how you view your properties, your data, and your entire operation."

Kaylie nodded eagerly. "We're talking about a complete paradigm shift. You need to start seeing your buildings as more than physical assets—as complex, data-generating ecosystems. Are you prepared to challenge everything you thought you knew about property operations and development?"

The challenge was indeed daunting. Were Vance and Vicki ready to question long-held assumptions and push beyond their comfort zone? Could they envision a future where data and digital infrastructures were as crucial to their success as bricks and mortar?

The two owners shared a look before turning back to the consultants. "We're ready," Vance said, his voice firm. "What's our first move?"

Dave smiled, a glint of excitement in his eyes. "Your first move is to prepare for a deep dive. We're going to take you through every system, every data point, every contract. We'll uncover inefficiencies you never knew existed and opportunities you never imagined possible."

"Bring it on!" Vicki cried, her competitive spirit fully ignited. "We didn't build this company by shying away from challenges. If this is what it takes to build a real estate dynasty, then that's what we'll do."

As they left the office that evening, Vance and Vicki knew the next morning would mark the beginning of a whole new ballgame in their real estate career. The question was no longer whether they were ready to take the leap, but how high they could soar.

CHAPTER 1 TAKEAWAYS

1. Challenge the status quo. Be prepared to question long-held assumptions and push beyond your comfort zone to revolutionize your property operations.

2. Clarity is key. Understanding your data and digital infrastructures is crucial for unlocking your properties' full potential. Use the DDIA tool to gain a comprehensive view of your assets.

3. Consolidate for success. Understand how the six key areas of digital infrastructure work together to create an intelligent building ecosystem.

4. Ask the right questions. Uncover hidden value and drive improvements by asking the five game-changing questions about each of the digital tools in your arsenal.

5. Take ownership of your data. Ensure you own and can access the data generated by your systems to create new value and revenue streams.

6. Know your playing field. Recognize the distinct challenges and opportunities inherent in brownfield and greenfield projects and tailor your strategy accordingly.

7. Embrace the paradigm shift. View your properties not just as physical assets but as complex, data-generating ecosystems with untapped potential.

TAKE ACTION

Complete the Data & Digital Infrastructure Audit (see appendix B) for your properties. This crucial step will provide the foundation for your transformation into a data-driven real estate champion.

CHAPTER 2

Connect: Developing Your Playbook

"Perfection is not attainable, but if we chase
perfection we can catch excellence."

—Vince Lombardi, five-time Super Bowl champion
coach of the Green Bay Packers

EXPANDING YOUR FIELD OF VISION

Vance stepped out of his car, squinting up at the ten-story office building that loomed before him. This downtown property had always been an important part of the Victors Real Estate Group portfolio, but now—armed with the insights from Dave and Kaylie of OpticWise—he saw it with a fresh eye.

Walking through the lobby, Vance noticed the security cameras and couldn't help but wonder about the networks they were running on. *How many networks are in here? How much are we paying for them each month?* he thought.

A few minutes later, Vance found himself in a small, stuffy room filled with blinking lights and humming equipment. The building engineer, Tom, was explaining the property's systems.

"This here's our HVAC control system," Tom said, pointing to a monitor. "And over there's our access control—"

"Tom," Vance interrupted, "how many separate networks are we running here?"

Tom scratched his head. "Well, let's see. There's one for HVAC, one for security, one for the leasing office . . . probably about eight or nine in total."

Vance's eyes widened. "Eight networks? For one building?"

Meanwhile, across town, Vicki stood on an empty plot of land, clutching blueprints for their planned apartment complex in her hands. "Before we start digging, I want to rethink our entire approach to the building's digital infrastructure," she said, turning to the project engineer beside her. "We have a chance to do this right from the ground up."

Surrounded by her project team, Vicki started walking through the planned layout.

"I want to know about every system we're planning to install," she continued. "Who will own the network it runs on? Who will own the data? How will we access it? And most important, how can we design a unified digital infrastructure to reduce both our build costs and our long-term operating expenses?"

Suddenly, Vicki noticed something on the blueprints.

"Hold on," she exclaimed, pointing to the blueprints, where several small rooms were scattered throughout the building. "Are all of these data closets?"

The lead architect nodded. "Yes, we typically allocate space for multiple network closets per floor to ensure connectivity throughout the building."

Vicki frowned, remembering Dave's words about efficiency. "How many do we actually need? It seems like we're using a lot of potentially rentable space for these closets."

The project engineer looked uncertain. "Well, traditionally, we've always—"

"'Traditionally' isn't good enough," Vicki interrupted. "I want us to review every single one of these. Let's figure out if we can consolidate our networks and reduce the number of these closets. Every square foot counts."

The team appeared taken aback, and Vicki knew they were surprised by her new perspective. She smiled, realizing how much her conversation with Dave and Kaylie had already expanded her outlook and changed her approach.

"We have an opportunity here to build smarter, not just bigger," she explained. "Let's make sure we're taking advantage of it."

As Vance and Vicki delved deeper into their respective projects, they began to uncover a wealth of inefficiencies and missed opportunities. They realized that developing a winning playbook for their properties would require a whole new approach to their systems, data, and digital infrastructure.

This was just the beginning of their journey from average performers to real estate champions.

Chapter 2 Goals

This chapter introduces your game plan for connecting and optimizing digital systems, guiding you through the Connect stage of the 5C process. You'll learn to harness the power of connecting disparate systems, transforming isolated frameworks into a unified powerhouse. We'll guide you through mastering both individual and collective system performance.

You'll discover our Five-Factor Prioritization Approach, a game-changing tool for strategic decision-making. We'll show you how to tailor strategies for existing properties and new developments alike. You'll learn to embrace agility, ensuring your digital strategy stays ahead of the curve.

By the chapter's end, you'll be equipped to create a unified digital nervous system for your properties, setting the stage for championship-level performance in commercial real estate.

CONNECTING THE DOTS

As Vance and Vicki began deep-diving into their respective properties, they uncovered a common thread: disconnection. The isolated systems and inefficiencies they found weren't just minor issues; they represented significant opportunities for improvement. In the world of commercial real estate, these disconnects are where the potential for transformation can be found.

Just as a championship sports team relies on seamless coordination between players, a high-performing property depends on the connections among—and the assimilation of—its various technological components. This assimilation happens on two levels: individual and coordinated.

Individual System Performance

At the most fundamental level, the success of an individual athlete depends on ensuring that their body is in top condition—their spine is aligned, their respiratory and nervous systems are functioning properly, and all their muscles and joints are in the best shape possible and working in concert with one another. This allows the athlete's body to coordinate all the complex movements required for peak performance.

In a building, this is analogous to each individual system—from HVAC to security to lighting to access controls and more—operating at its optimal level. Each distinct system must be properly maintained, updated, and configured to perform its specific function efficiently and effectively.

Systems Coordination

For a sports team, however, each player performing at their individual best is not enough. Success comes only when all players work together cohesively, utilizing the same playbook. This coordinated effort allows the team to achieve results far beyond what any individual player could accomplish alone.

Similarly, in property operations, the goal is to ensure all systems are not only performing optimally on their own but also working together in concert. This means creating a shared framework—a **unified digital infrastructure**—where all connected systems can communicate, share data, and operate harmoniously to achieve optimal results for the entire property.

This is precisely the goal in property operations: ensuring all systems are prepared to perform at their individual best while coming together on a shared framework and contributing to a shared **data repository** to achieve optimal results for the entire property.

Harnessing the Power of Your Systems

Just as a well-coordinated sports team can adapt to changing game conditions, an integrated building system can respond more effectively to changing occupancy patterns, energy requirements, WiFi demands, security needs, and so forth. The first step in developing this shared playbook is to identify and connect all of your digital assets (software, hardware, and data sources). This process is akin to creating a **digital backbone** for your property—a singular, interconnected infrastructure that ensures everything is aligned, connected, and working together efficiently.

Remember, data and digital i nfrastructures include all of your hardware and software as well as the data sources they generate across the six key areas of digital infrastructure outlined in chapter 1:

Network infrastructure and IoT

Security, access control, and risk management

Energy, environmental management, and sustainability

Property operations and tenant experience

Financial and asset management

Data aggregation and analytics

Now that you've worked with your team to complete the Data & Digital Infrastructure Audit (appendix B), you have gained clarity on all the digital hardware, software, and data sources you have in place. The next step is to ensure they're all up and running, connected, and delivering data that you own in order to build out a championship playbook.

Every operations system in a building is a potential data source. To truly harness the power of these systems, property owners need to ask three key questions:

1. Who owns the system and its data? This question is crucial because data ownership directly impacts your ability to leverage information for decision-making and value creation. If a vendor owns your data, you may face restrictions on how you can use it or even access it. This limits your ability to generate insights and optimize your property's performance.

2. How can we access the data? Understanding data accessibility is vital for ensuring you can actually use the information your systems generate. Even if you do own the data, difficulties or delays in access, or going through a third party, can slow down your decision-making process. That puts you at a serious disadvantage when changing conditions or opportunities require a quick response.

3. Is it a push or a pull system for data retrieval? The method of data retrieval and the granularity of data that the system provides impact the timeliness and efficiency of your data usage.

    > **Push systems** automatically send, log, or post data to a central repository, allowing for near real-time monitoring and quick responses.

    > **Pull systems** allow you to request data and can provide extensive, templatized datasets.

Understanding which methods each system supports helps you plan your data management strategy effectively.

However, it's not just about the data. The physical connections between systems are equally important. Many buildings operate multiple, separate networks. Like the inefficient, illogical, uneconomical choice to charter multiple planes to transport each player separately to an away game, running multiple disconnected networks increases costs, complicates both maintenance and data exchanges, and reduces overall system efficiency.

In his downtown building, Vance discovered eight separate networks for different systems, with each network requiring its own maintenance, security measures, and dedicated space. This is highly inefficient! Vicki faced a similar reality when reviewing the blueprints for their new apartment complex. By consolidating isolated networks into a single, robust digital infrastructure, property owners can significantly reduce costs, simplify management, free up rentable square footage, and expose new opportunities for system coordination and data analysis with artificial intelligence (see chapter 4 for more on AI).

Moreover, a unified digital infrastructure allows for easier implementation of building-wide policies, better security management, accurate documentation and equipment tracking, and more comprehensive data analysis. On a sports team, it's the difference between each player following their own strategy and building a cohesive unit that works from the same playbook toward a common goal.

GOOD SPORTS: We Are the Champions[7]

The US Women's National Team (USWNT)—in particular, their journey from their shocking 2023 World Cup exit to Olympic gold in 2024—offers a powerful lesson in the importance of connection and agility. Connection and agility are essential principles in any effort to lift one's performance to the highest possible level, just as crucial in commercial real estate as they are on the soccer field.

Under Coach Vlatko Andonovski in 2023, the USWNT boasted some of the most talented and decorated players in women's soccer history. The roster included legends like Megan Rapinoe, Alex Morgan, and Julie Ertz alongside rising stars such as Sophia Smith and Trinity Rodman. Despite this wealth of individual talent, the team struggled with disconnection. Players felt unprepared and tense, unable to perform at their best.

The team's tactics were criticized as reductive and inflexible. Critics suggested they were failing to adapt to the evolving methods of their global competition. In the round of 16 World Cup

---

7   Kellen Becoats, "Where Did It All Go Wrong for the USWNT?" The Ringer, August 7, 2023, https://www.theringer.com/2023/08/07/soccer/uswnt-vs-sweden-analysis-what-went-wrong-womens-world-cup; Jeff Carlisle, "Does the 2023 World Cup Signal the End of USWNT Dominance?" ESPN, August 9, 2023, https://www.espn.com/soccer/story/_/page/uswntreport0809/uswnt-soccer-dominance-world-cup-2023-exit; Chantel Jennings, "'This Team Has Gone Through a Lot': How the USWNT Overcame a Year of Change to Win Olympic Gold," The Athletic, August 10, 2024; Ryan Tolmich, "'It's Just Love'—How the Irrepressible Emma Hayes Resurrected the USWNT, Restored the Faith and Turned Tarnish into Gold," Goal.com, August 13, 2024, https://www.goal.com/en-us/lists/uswnt-emma-hayes-olympics/bltbccfd6d347c01006; Alex Windley, "4 Reasons Why the USWNT Failed at the 2023 Women's World Cup," Bleacher Report, August 6, 2023, https://bleacherreport.com/articles/10085262-4-reasons-why-the-uswnt-failed-at-the-2023-womens-world-cup.

continued

matches against Sweden, the team's rigidity led to their earliest World Cup exit ever, when late and limited substitutions left them unable to break the deadlock. The mismatch between the team's potential and its performance was stark and surprising.

This scenario mirrors the pitfalls of disconnected systems in commercial real estate. Like the USWNT's world-class individual talents who weren't effectively integrated, buildings with top-tier but isolated systems fail to reach their full potential. And like the team's inability to adapt tactics mid-game, inflexible building management systems can't respond to changing occupancy patterns, maintenance needs, or energy demands, even when equipped with cutting-edge technology.

Enter new US head coach Emma Hayes in 2024. In just seventy-nine days, Hayes transformed the team's approach, emphasizing connection and agility. She rebuilt the program around a core of young, dynamic players while strategically utilizing experienced veterans. Hayes fostered an environment where players could enjoy their game, leading to more creative and adaptive play on the field. The result, achieved through a series of hard-fought victories where different players stepped up at crucial moments, was Olympic gold.

This transformation parallels the potential of well-integrated, agile digital systems in commercial real estate—building management systems that respond quickly to challenges and allow for real-time adjustments. This approach can lead to significant improvements in efficiency, tenant satisfaction, NOI, and overall property value.

In both sports and real estate, success stems from more than just talented individuals or advanced technologies. It comes from creating a connected, responsive system that is able to seize opportunities as they arise.

When properly integrated, the whole can indeed be greater than the sum of its parts.

> ## Key Takeaways for Real Estate
>
> Like the USWNT under Emma Hayes, successful real estate operators need to:
> - Foster connection between different systems and teams.
> - Embrace agility and adaptability in operations.
> - Balance experienced systems with innovative new technologies.
> - Develop an environment that encourages creativity and enjoyment in problem-solving.

A STATE OF PLAY

New USWNT head coach Emma Hayes approached her team with creativity, playfulness, and an open mind. Successful coaches emphasize the joy of engaging in this process—a principle that translates well to property operations. Property owners should embrace a similar mindset as they move from the inventory process (see chapter 1) toward connecting and aligning all their digital systems. Delving deeper into their systems, they are likely to uncover surprising (yet common) insights—one of the most exciting parts of this work.

Let's explore what may come to light when you start optimizing your property's digital systems.

Vendor Consolidation

Due to market consolidation, you might be purchasing multiple systems from the same vendor, potentially giving you more negotiating power. For example, Vicki discovered that after recent mergers, the same company would be providing all the security cameras, access control, and parking management systems for the new apartment complex. This revelation allowed her to renegotiate VRE's contracts with the vendor, resulting in a 15 percent cost reduction across all three services.

System Redundancy

A newer, more comprehensive system may be available to replace multiple older systems, reducing both complexity and cost. Vicki found that the new building management system lined up for the apartment complex could integrate HVAC control, lighting management, and energy monitoring—functions typically handled by three separate systems. This integration could potentially reduce the property's technology footprint by 30 percent and streamline operations significantly.

Underutilized Services

You might already be paying for services or features that you're not fully utilizing. Tom (the building engineer) admitted to Vance that the downtown property was using only the most basic of the HVAC management system's capabilities. By fully leveraging the system's features, VRE could reduce energy consumption by an additional 10 percent to 15 percent.

Outdated Pricing

When was the last time your CRE team reviewed your properties' service contracts? If contracts haven't been reviewed in years, you're likely overpaying for some services. Vance's team found that the elevator maintenance contract for the ten-story office building had not changed in seven years. Due to annual, automatic escalations, that vendor was now charging rates nearly 30 percent above current market prices. Renegotiating this one contract alone promised to save VRE thousands of dollars annually.

Workflow Improvements

Some systems might allow for remote management, reducing the need for on-site personnel. For example, Vicki identified a modern access control system that would allow for remote monitoring and management of building entry, potentially eliminating the need for one 24/7 security guard and saving over $100,000 annually in costs.

Dormant Smart Systems

Were expensive smart systems installed in your CRE property but never properly activated or utilized? Tom showed Vance a sophisticated lighting control system that was never fully implemented after being installed four years earlier. Activating this dormant system reduced energy consumption for lighting by up to 35 percent.

Approaching systems assimilation and optimization with curiosity can lead to innovative solutions and yield unexpected benefits. Property owners who take inventory of their data and digital infrastructure can discover untapped potential in their existing systems and contracts, allowing them to integrate various building systems into a connected, efficient whole. These discoveries—and the ability to create a cohesive unit from disparate parts—mirror the approach of great coaches across various sports, who uncover hidden talents in overlooked players and find new ways to utilize veterans.

The goal isn't just to cut costs or increase efficiency, but to create a more responsive, adaptable, and enjoyable property for your residents and employees. Property owners who adopt this open-minded, curious, and playful mindset can move beyond a solid property that's simply a collection of systems, to create a unified, agile entity that can adapt to changing needs and maximize its championship potential.

PRIORITIZE WINS: A STRATEGIC FIVE-FACTOR APPROACH

Now that you've documented and clarified all of your digital systems—hardware, software, and data sources—you might be feeling overwhelmed. This is normal, especially when evaluating larger properties where complexity can quickly multiply. Remember, this complexity represents a web of opportunities to develop championship properties. However, we can't tackle everything at once. We need to prioritize.

In the world of commercial real estate, strategic prioritization is akin to a coach developing a game plan for leading the team to victory. A coach prioritizes plays based on the team's strengths, the opponent's weaknesses, and the particular game situation. Just as a coach can't implement every possible play in a single game, a manager can't overhaul every system simultaneously. When the goal is to transform a property into a high-performing asset, property owners and managers must prioritize improvements based on their property's current status, market demands, and the potential return on investment.

To help make these crucial decisions, we've developed the Five-Factor Prioritization Approach as follows.

1. OpEx. Begin with the most costly systems and networks, listed by operating expenses. OpEx includes annual support, upgrades, maintenance, and any other related costs. If it's a new build, also do an ROI analysis to determine the payback period. For example, in Vance's downtown office building, he discovered eight separate networks for different systems. By prioritizing the consolidation of these networks, he could realize significant savings in maintenance costs and free up capital required for future upgrades.

2. Performance. Next, focus on "high touch" systems, which are often the pain points in your operation—those that require significant personnel time or frequent troubleshooting. Furthermore, any time your staff serves as the control mechanism, evaluate the actual expense of maintaining this human-dependent system compared with automated options. If the HVAC system in Vicki's new building requires constant attention from the building engineer and causes frequent tenant complaints, this would be a high-priority area for improvement.

3. Data ownership. Identify systems that don't give you access to your own data. In today's digital age, data is a valuable asset, and you should control yours. As discussed in chapter 1, it's your building, and those are your tenants—thus, it's your data. If the access control system in Vance's office building is managed by a third-party vendor that owns all the usage data, this could be a priority area. Vance's team should focus on gaining full access to all of their data—in this case, it's the valuable information that is generated every time someone enters or exits a space.

4. Digital infrastructure ownership. Determine who owns the physical networks and hardware within your property. Owning your digital infrastructure gives you more control and often leads to cost savings—both CapEx and OpEx. In Vicki's new apartment complex project, ensuring that the building owns and controls its network infrastructure from the outset prevents her company from paying for multiple networks to be built and maintained.

5. Time sensitivity. Finally, consider contract expiration dates, essential upgrades, and any regulatory requirements on the horizon. The elevator maintenance contract in Vance's office building is up for renewal in three months, presenting a time-sensitive opportunity to reassess the current arrangement and negotiate better terms or explore the potential efficiencies of open data systems.

By evaluating each system against these five factors, property owners can start to craft a playbook well-suited for any property in any context. Like a great coach, you want to approach this process with an open mind and an eye toward high-leverage plays, focusing strategically on the digital systems that will have the most significant impact on your property's performance.

Remember, just as a skilled coach adjusts their strategy based on the flow of the game, you should be prepared to adapt your priorities as you gather more information and as market conditions change. As always, the goal is to create a dynamic, responsive approach to property operations that keeps you ahead of the competition and delivers championship-level results.

EYES ON THE PRIZE

As the USWNT's transformation proves, having a clear strategy and the right approach can turn a struggling team into champions. In commercial real estate, tools like our Data and Digital Infrastructure Prioritization Chart (see Figure 4 and appendix E) can help keep your eyes on the prize, focusing on the biggest and best plays that will take your properties to the next level.

This tool ranks systems and data sources based on the five high-priority factors, informing you about what to tackle next with your team. Use it to identify which "players" (systems) need attention and how best to utilize them. The systems with the highest total scores should be your top priorities. Figure 4 illustrates this process with the first of the Data and Digital Infrastructure domains, network infrastructure and IoT.

Figure 4. Data and Digital Infrastructure Prioritization Chart

DDI Domain & Element	ROI	Performance Issues	Data Ownership	Infrastructure Ownership	Time Sensitivity	Total Score
Network Infrastructure and IoT	☑ 1	☑ 1	☑ 1	☑ 1	☑ 1	Sum =
• Asset tracking systems	2	2	2	2	2	
• Common area WiFi	3	3	3	3	3	
• Internet circuit(s)	4	4	4	4	4	
• Financial and Asset Management	5	5	5	5	5	
• Occupancy sensors						
• Smart technology						
• Temperature and humdity sensors						
• Tenant spaces WiFi						
• Voice services						

Each system is rated on a scale of 1 to 5 for each factor, with 5 being the highest priority. Here's what these numbers mean:

Return on investment

- 1 = Low potential for cost savings or revenue generation.
- 5 = High potential for significant financial impact.

Performance issues

- 1 = System works well with minimal issues.
- 5 = System frequently causes problems or inefficiencies.

Data ownership

- 1 = You have full ownership of and access to your data.
- 5 = Data is entirely vendor-controlled, with limited access.

Infrastructure ownership

- 1 = You own and control the digital infrastructure.
- 5 = The digital infrastructure is entirely vendor-owned and -managed.

Time sensitivity

- 1 = No urgent need for changes.
- 5 = Immediate action required (e.g., contract expiring, compliance issues).

By using this tool as part of their playbook, property owners can transform their approach to digital management. This prioritization process is crucial for both brownfield and greenfield projects, though the application differs:

- For existing properties (brownfield projects), focus on optimizing current systems to increase income. This could involve reducing OpEx or finding new revenue streams. For example, Vance might prioritize consolidating the eight separate networks in his office building, potentially saving on maintenance costs and identifying new services to sell to tenants.

- For new developments (greenfield projects), work with engineers from the start to reduce build costs (CapEx) and design an optimal digital infrastructure to minimize OpEx. Vicki's decision to rethink the apartment complex's digital infrastructure before construction begins is a perfect example of this strategy.

In both cases, the key is to expand beyond CRE's traditional metrics like occupancy rates and financials. Using tools like this chart and the DDIA to gain a comprehensive understanding of their properties and how to improve them, owners can develop new revenue streams, reduce expenses, and increase the value realized by all stakeholders.

This detail-oriented approach to property operations requires constant evolution and adaptation. Sticking with outdated systems or uncooperative vendors is like a coach refusing to adapt their strategy even when it's clearly not working. Every sports fan has been baffled by a coach who never updates their playbook, runs the same play over and over again, and continues to lose. As the old saying goes, *Insanity is doing the same thing over and over again and expecting different results.* Truly great coaches and athletes look beyond conventional tactics and player roles. Rather than rely on past successes or outdated strategies, they continually analyze, adapt, and innovate. To be successful, CRE operators must likewise be willing to reassess and update their methods regularly.

This includes being ready to let a vendor or digital system go if they're not adding value to your property or not playing by your rules. These entities should work for you and your property—not the other way around. If a vendor is unwilling to revise or revisit a contract according to your needs, or to let you aggregate your data outside of their system, it's time to tear that page out of your playbook.

In the pursuit of a more connected property, sometimes separating from the status quo—whether that means removing outdated systems or parting ways with vendors that aren't delivering value or acknowledging your new data requirements—is the best move. While change can seem risky, staying with restrictive, redundant, or antiquated systems often means sacrificing control or insight (or both) and missing out on potential benefits.

Remember the golden rule of the digital age: In your property, every digital system and piece of data should be owned by you, with data stored in your data lake and working toward your goals. By keeping your eyes on the prize—a fully optimized, efficient, and profitable property—and using tools like the Data and Digital Infrastructure Prioritization Chart, you can rethink your digital strategy, reimagine your team's approach, and lead your properties to new heights of success.

A PLAYBOOK FOR PEAK PERFORMANCE

After a week focused on their respective properties, Vance and Vicki felt like they had just completed an intense training session. Their minds were buzzing with new information, and their bodies ached from walking the length, width, and height of their buildings while inspecting every nook and cranny.

Vicki had truly embraced this process, striving to make it fun and personal for her team. "How can we inject soul into our spaces?" she asked. "What services can we add onto this large asset instead of simply seeing it as rentable space?"

When the time came to reconvene with Dave and Kaylie in VRE's conference room, Vicki and Vance brought with them a pile of notes and diagrams as well as a newfound sense of purpose. They had spent the day applying their new DDIA to their properties, uncovering a wealth of opportunities: Vance had identified over $100,000 in potential annual savings by consolidating networks and renegotiating vendor contracts in their office building. Meanwhile, Vicki had worked with their architects to redesign the plans for their new apartment complex, significantly increasing rentable space while reducing build costs by a few percentage points. Both identified new revenue opportunities.

The whiteboard that once held their portfolio's basic **key performance indicators (KPIs)** now displayed a complex web of digital systems, data flows, and potential optimizations. Vance's eyes kept darting to the eight different sketches of network diagrams for their ten-story downtown office building. He was still in disbelief. "I can't believe we've been missing so much potential," he said, gesturing at the artifacts displayed on the wall.

Vicki nodded, her gaze fixed on the apartment complex blueprints spread across the table. "And to think we were about to build a whole new property with the same inefficiencies," she added, circling several unnecessary data closets with a red marker.

Dave knew these two were on the championship path. "This is just the beginning," he pointed out. "You've taken the first crucial steps in seeing your properties with fresh eyes."

Kaylie pointed to the prioritization charts they had created together. "By ranking your systems based on ROI, performance issues, data ownership, infrastructure ownership, and time sensitivity, you've created a roadmap for optimization. But implementing these changes will require a team effort."

Vicki nodded. "You're right. We can't do this alone. We need a team, from our property managers to our partners to our operations staff, that understands this new approach."

Vance agreed, "It's not just about hiring a data scientist; it's about getting everyone on board with this new way of thinking. We need to build a data-driven culture across our entire organization."

Dave leaned in. "That's exactly right. And that's where we'll focus next. Building the right team is crucial to turning these insights into reality."

As they packed up for the night, Vance turned to Dave and Kaylie. "So, what's our next move? How do we start building this team?"

Kaylie jumped into the discussion. "We'll need to reassess your entire organizational structure. You'll need to train or add people who see the big picture and understand how all these systems work together. And you'll rely on staff who are adaptable, ready to learn new skills and take on new roles."

Dave added, "Remember, you're not just in the real estate business anymore. You're in the data business and the business of building championship properties. The team you build to do that will be the foundation of your success."

CHAPTER 2 TAKEAWAYS

1. Harness the power of connection. Understand how integrating disparate systems can transform your property's performance, mirroring the success of championship sports teams.

2. Optimize individual and collective performance. Learn to fine-tune each digital system while creating a harmonious, unified digital infrastructure.

3. Master data ownership and accessibility. Discover key questions to ask about your data and digital infrastructure, unlocking valuable insights.

4. Prioritize strategically. Implement our Five-Factor Prioritization Approach to focus your efforts where they'll have the most impact.

5. Tailor your approach. Understand the unique strategies needed for existing properties (brownfield) versus new developments (greenfield).

6. Stay agile and adaptable. Recognize the importance of regularly reassessing and updating your digital strategy to stay ahead of the competition.

7. Foster a winning mindset. Approach your digital transformation with curiosity and openness, embracing the process of discovery and improvement. Learn to ask the right questions about your systems and data, challenging the status quo to uncover hidden opportunities.

TAKE ACTION

Use the Data and Digital Infrastructure Prioritization Chart in appendix E to build a spreadsheet that will allow you to assess and rank your existing systems. Then, starting with your highest-priority items, begin developing your playbook for digital transformation.

CHAPTER 3

Collect: Building the Best Team

"The strength of the team is each individual member.
The strength of each member is the team."

—Phil Jackson, NBA champion (New York Knicks) and eleven-time
NBA championship coach (Chicago Bulls, Los Angeles Lakers)

TRANSFORMATION STARTS AT THE TOP

Vance and Vicki were riding high on their newfound enthusiasm for data-driven property operations. After completing the Data & Digital Infrastructure Audit recommended by Dave and Kaylie, suddenly they were seeing their portfolio with absolute clarity from the best seats in the house.

The audit had revealed numerous opportunities for optimization, from consolidating redundant networks to leveraging dormant smart systems. Insights from the Data and Digital Infrastructure Prioritization Chart, supported by the Five-Factor Prioritization Approach, had helped Vance and Vicki begin to develop a winning strategy as the foundation of their playbook. Equipped with this new clarity, they were eager to transform their properties into high-performing, inter-connected assets.

Now it was time to build the right offense and team to make it happen.

As they were discussing their next steps, Vance's phone buzzed loudly. It was an email notification from MegaProp Solutions, a very large, well-known real estate services firm.

"Vicki, look at this," Vance said. "MegaProp wants to meet with us. They say they can upgrade our internet, network, and WiFi at this site."

Vicki raised an eyebrow. "Really? What exactly are they offering?"

Vance scrolled through the email. "They're promising to bring in new backbone circuits, upgrade WiFi services, and implement something called the CONNECT app that should tie in access, HVAC, cameras, events, and conference room scheduling. It sounds comprehensive."

The couple decided to take the meeting. A few days later, they arrived in a conference room that looked like it could be an exhibit in New York's Museum of Modern Art. They sat facing a team of pol-ished MegaProp executives.

The lead executive began her pitch. "At MegaProp, we understand that effective and resilient networks are increasingly important given the growing reliance on connectivity and digital innovations in the industry."

A second exec chimed in. "Our network advisory services group helps organizations navigate the dynamic landscape of network tech-nology to negotiate agreements and maximize cost savings while increasing reliability and optimizing performance."

The presentation continued, outlining how MegaProp could transform the Victors Real Estate Group portfolio with cutting-edge technology by leveraging its global network of expertise and affiliated companies.

Leaving the meeting an hour later, Vicki turned to Vance. "That was . . . overwhelming. But they seem to have everything figured out. Maybe this group can make things simpler for us."

Vance was a bit shell-shocked. "I know. Maybe we should thank OpticWise for getting us started, but leave this stuff to MegaProp. They claim to be experts."

Yet something didn't sit right with them. They knew from experience that bigger is not always better. They decided to run the proposal by Dave and Kaylie before deciding on the next steps.

The next day, they met with the OpticWise team. As Dave and Kaylie reviewed MegaProp's proposal, their expressions grew increasingly concerned.

"Vance, Vicki," Dave began carefully, "I know this proposal looks impressive. MegaProp is big, but there are some serious red flags."

Kaylie nodded. "MegaProp is primarily a brokerage firm. They don't actually operate any digital infrastructures for their clients. In this proposal, they're essentially technology services brokers, getting commissions for recommending vendors that ultimately pay them a revenue share of the services you buy."

"Look at their promise of 'favorable pricing and terms,'" Dave added. "In reality, MegaProp is negotiating service contracts, which means they get paid but aren't accountable for deliverables or the user experience."

Vicki frowned. "But they're offering this CONNECT app that seems to tie everything together. Isn't that good?"

"It might seem convenient," Kaylie replied. "And it may connect to some systems, assuming you upgrade multiple systems to the platforms they recommend. Even then, it's limited to tenant and employee engagement. It's not bringing all of your independently capable operations systems into a cohesive data and digital infrastructure."

She explained that Vicki and Vance would be locked into MegaProp's commercial ecosystem—which VRE likely wouldn't wholly own—for the length of the contract. And they would still have plenty of fragmented data sources.

"If you ever want to switch property managers," Kaylie continued, "you'll be stuck with their vendors, systems, and service agreements."

Dave leaned forward. "Remember what we discussed about data ownership? MegaProp's model often involves them and their vendors controlling your data and infrastructure. You'd be giving away one of your most valuable assets—your data."

Vance and Vicki sat back, stunned. The glossy proposal from MegaProp suddenly seemed less appealing.

"So, what do you suggest?" Vance asked.

"A successful partnership starts with your entire team accepting the importance of a culture built around owning your data and digital infrastructure," Dave warned. "If an organization or individual on your team doesn't care about that, it's not going to work."

As Vance and Vicki left their meeting with Dave and Kaylie, they felt exhilarated but overwhelmed. The potential of data-driven property operations was clear, but the path to get there seemed daunting. How could they be sure everyone in the organization—including their outside vendors—was on the same page?

"It's like we've been playing checkers all this time, and now we're learning chess," Vance mused as they walked back to their office. "We have to understand how all the players on the board intend to act."

Vicki nodded, her brow furrowed in thought. "We have to transform our entire organization, top to bottom, into a data powerhouse. But where do we even start?"

Their question echoes the challenge faced by many in the commercial real estate industry. When you're striving to create a successful CRE organization centered on unified data and digital infrastructures, everyone involved has to be on the same page. Transformation must start at the top—with leadership fully committed to the new approach.

Chapter 3 Goals

This chapter will guide you through Collect—the third critical C in the journey to building a championship-level commercial real estate organization. Winning teams gather the right athletes and get them working together on the best offensive strategy. You'll do the same thing with your team by assembling, owning, and uniting your data and digital infrastructure for peak performance.

Now that you've connected all of your data sources, we'll help you collect all of your data in a single location that you own and control. In this chapter, we'll explore the critical components of the CRE "triangle offense"—process, people, and technology—and show you how to collect these pieces into a winning strategy. You'll learn how to cultivate a data-driven culture that permeates every level of your company, from the C-suite to maintenance staff.

You'll also continue to discover the importance of data ownership and how to negotiate effectively with vendors to ensure you maintain control of your most valuable assets. By the end of this chapter, you'll understand how to collect and organize your resources into a cohesive system that gives you a competitive edge in the market.

DEVELOPING A DATA-POWERED DYNASTY

Building a championship-level, data-driven organization requires more than just acquiring properties and managing them traditionally. It demands a fundamental shift in thinking—a move toward a data-driven culture that permeates every level of the organization.

Let's consider the five critical areas where owning both your data and your digital infrastructure can elevate your real estate game.

1. Improved Decision-Making

By leveraging data analytics, your property operations team can make more informed choices about space utilization, systems optimizations, property improvements, and much more. Imagine being able to predict with certainty that adding a specific amenity would increase tenant retention rates, or to calculate what adjustments would reduce utility expenses. That's the power of data-driven decision-making.

2. Optimized Operations

In every one of the six key data and digital infrastructure domains, there are critical operations that can be streamlined, improved, or even eliminated. Some teams approach one domain at a time, looking for improvements in each area. Take, for example, the energy and resource management domain—one real estate firm found that by analyzing energy consumption data, they were able to reduce utility costs by a whopping 22 percent across their portfolio. That's not just good for the bottom line—it's a significant step toward more sustainable operations.

Figure 5. Leadership at Every Level: Power Plays for Developing a Data-Driven Culture

Leadership Level	Power Play
C-Suite	**Lead by example.** Regularly reference data in decision-making processes and strategic discussions. **Invest in data infrastructure.** Allocate resources for data collection, storage, and analysis. **Set data-driven goals.** Establish KPIs that require data analysis to measure and achieve.
Middle Management	**Implement training programs.** Offer regular training sessions on data analysis tools and techniques. **Incorporate data-driven performance reviews.** Infuse data usage and analysis skills into performance evaluations. **Create cross-functional data teams.** Bring together individuals from different departments to collaborate on data projects.
Property Manager	**Encourage daily data rituals.** Start each day by reviewing key data points from the properties. **Create data challenge programs.** Develop friendly competitions where managers use data to solve real property issues. **Develop mentorship programs.** Match data-savvy managers with those less experienced to foster peer-to-peer learning.
Maintenance and Operations	**Train on IoT.** Train staff on using IoT devices and interpreting the data they produce. **Implement data-driven maintenance schedules.** Employ predictive maintenance based on equipment performance data. **Train in prompt engineering.** Train staff on how to use AI prompts for the best results. **Establish feedback loops.** Build systems for staff to report data discrepancies or suggest new data points to track.
Leasing and Sales Teams	**Pitch with data.** Train teams to incorporate data insights into their property pitches and negotiations. **Provide market analysis tools.** Provide access to comprehensive market data tools and training on their effective use. **Use performance tracking.** Use data to track and improve individual and team performance metrics.

3. Enhanced Tenant Experience

One of the most intriguing aspects of a data-driven approach is its potential to enhance the tenant experience. By analyzing foot traffic patterns, usage of common areas, and tenant feedback data, property managers can tailor their services to better meet tenant needs. One major office complex saw a 30 percent increase in tenant satisfaction scores after implementing this approach.

4. Predictive Maintenance

Imagine being able to anticipate equipment failures before they happen, minimizing downtime and reducing repair costs. That's exactly what data from IoT sensors can help you achieve. Implementing a predictive maintenance system across your real estate portfolio means your team can analyze data from sensors on HVAC systems, elevators, and other critical equipment, and then schedule maintenance proactively. One property management company reduced unexpected downtime by 38 percent and slashed maintenance costs by nearly 20 percent.

5. Increased NOI = Higher Valuations

The benefits of a data-driven approach don't stop at operations. In the world of commercial real estate, property valuation is a focal point for everything from investment decisions to loan applications, and net operating income is the common driving force behind it all. Net operating income (NOI) can be positively impacted by increasing revenues or decreasing expenses, both of which are results of data and digital infrastructure ownership.

Furthermore, when you incorporate a wide range of data points—from local market trends to detailed operational inputs—valuations become more accurate and defensible. One real estate investment trust (REIT) using this data-driven valuation method was able to increase their portfolio value by a few percentage points during their quarterly assessment.

Of course, the transition to a data-driven culture isn't always smooth sailing. As Vance and Vicki contemplated the challenges ahead, they realized they needed to cultivate a winning culture in their organization. This reminded them of an unlikely success story—one that proves that with the right strategy and team, even the most daunting odds can be overcome.

They called it the "Miracle on Ice."

GOOD SPORTS: Mindful of Miracles[8]

The 1980 US Olympic hockey team's "Miracle on Ice" wasn't just an upset—it was a seismic shock in sports history that offers powerful lessons for commercial real estate leaders aiming to build data-driven organizations.

Consider the odds: The Soviet team had dominated international hockey for two decades, winning gold medals at the previous

---

8   Emily Kaplan and Greg Wyshynski, "NHL Viewers Club: 'Miracle,' the Story of the 1980 USA Hockey Team," *ESPN*, May 22, 2020, https://www.espn.com/nhl/story/_/id/29200613/nhl-viewers-club-miracle-story-1980-usa-hockey-team; Chris Peters, "Inside the Miracle on Ice: How Team USA Defied the Numbers to Beat the Soviet Union at the 1980 Olympics," *ESPN*, February 19, 2020, https://www.espn.com/nhl/story/_/id/28701139/inside-miracle-ice-how-team-usa-defied-numbers-beat-soviet-union-1980-olympics; Dave Roos, "'Miracle on Ice': When the US Olympic Hockey Team Stunned the World," History.com, February 22, 2024, https://www.history.com/news/miracle-on-ice-hockey-olympic-game.

continued

four Olympic Games. They'd beaten the United States in all twelve meetings between 1960 and 1980, outscoring them 117–26. Just a week before the Olympics, the USSR walloped the USA 10–3 in an exhibition game. The American squad, composed of amateur college players with an average age of twenty-one, was given no chance against the Soviet professionals.

Yet against all expectations, Team USA emerged victorious in the medal round, beating the USSR 4–3 and going on to win the gold medal two days later. This David versus Goliath triumph parallels the potential for CRE firms to use data and strategy to compete against seemingly insurmountable odds.

Coach Herb Brooks implemented a hybrid playing style, combining North American physicality with European finesse. This mirrors how CRE organizations can blend traditional industry knowledge with cutting-edge data analytics to create a unique competitive advantage. His emphasis on rigorous conditioning reflects the need for robust data infrastructure in real estate operations. Crucially, Brooks and his staff meticulously analyzed opponent tendencies and adjusted tactics for each game. This data-driven flexibility is essential in today's dynamic real estate market.

But Coach Brooks's approach to team building was truly revolutionary. He didn't just select the most talented players; he chose those who best fit his innovative system. Similarly, CRE firms should build teams capable of leveraging data insights and cultivating a data-savvy culture across all roles.

Despite being outshot 39–16 by the Soviets in that famous game, the US team's strategic use of their resources led to victory—a powerful reminder that in CRE, it's not about having the most data, but using it most effectively. By embracing these principles, your CRE organization can achieve its own Miracle on Ice moment, transforming from an underdog to a market leader in the data-driven era.

Key Takeaways for Real Estate

Like the 1980 US men's hockey team, successful real estate operators need to:

- Refuse to be intimidated by large competitors or vendors—smart data use can level the playing field.
- Build a team that thrives in a data-driven environment.
- Blend traditional knowledge with innovative analytics.
- Continuously analyze market data to adjust strategies.
- Use data to efficiently allocate resources.

LEADING AT EVERY LEVEL

For Coach Herb Brooks to build a team capable of achieving the impossible, he had to lead by example and ensure every player was aligned with the team's vision. As his stunning approach showed, with the right team, strategy, and use of information, even the most formidable competitors can be overcome.

Now, Vance and Vicki had begun a similar journey of striving toward victory despite enormous challenges. At the leadership level of their organization, they would need to regularly reference data in their decision-making processes and strategic discussions. They would need to invest in data and digital infrastructure, allocating resources for data collection, storage, and analysis. And they would need to set data-driven goals, establishing KPIs that require data analysis to measure and achieve.

But it's not just about the C-suite. To truly cultivate a data-driven dynasty, every level of the organization needs to be involved. Middle managers need training programs and data-driven performance reviews. Property and operations managers need daily data rituals and long-term mentorship programs. Maintenance and operations staff need to be trained in using IoT devices and interpreting the data they produce.

The road ahead would indeed be challenging, but with the right offense, Vance and Vicki knew they could transform their CRE organization from an average performer into a true dynastic champion, capable of adapting to market changes and consistently outperforming their competitors. The game had changed, and they were ready to play.

Like the VRE team, your entire team needs to accept the importance of this concept in order to transition from traditional ownership, operations, and management to a holistic digital, data-driven approach. This shift is akin to moving from an old-school, gut-instinct coaching style to a modern, data- and analytics-driven approach in sports. And not everyone will automatically be on board with that type of change.

To overcome any resistance within your team, it's important to celebrate early wins and share success stories across the organization. For instance, when a manager uses data analysis to negotiate a more favorable OpEx renewal, resulting in a 7 percent decrease in operating costs, make sure this positive step is widely communicated and celebrated.

Sharing real-world examples with your people will help demonstrate the tangible benefits of your new, data-driven offense. Property owners must remember that they're not just in the real estate business anymore; they're in the data business. This shift in perspective is crucial for building a team and an offensive strategy that can truly leverage the power of data and digital infrastructures.

To foster this data-driven culture, leadership must implement specific strategies across all levels of the organization (see Figure 5). What might this look like in practice?

At the C-suite level, the CEO might start each board meeting with a data-driven insight that influenced a recent major decision.

At the middle management level, managers could be tasked with creating monthly reports that highlight key performance indicators derived from their property's data.

On the ground, maintenance staff could be equipped with tablets that allow them to utilize repair data in real time, contributing to the organization's predictive maintenance cost reduction efforts.

Initiating these small shifts in behavior and encouraging data-driven conversations are how you can build the necessary foundation from which to launch the big plays where your team's culture develops.

THE CRE TRIANGLE OFFENSE: PROCESS, PEOPLE, AND TECHNOLOGY

As Vance and Vicki contemplated the challenge of integrating data-driven practices across their entire organization, they realized they needed a framework that could bring together all the elements they had learned about. What strategy would unite their processes, people, and technology in order to build a dynamic, adaptable system?

In the end, they drew their inspiration from the world of basketball.

In the late 1980s and 1990s, Phil Jackson led Michael Jordan and the Chicago Bulls to six NBA championships using an innovative system known as the "triangle offense." This strategy wasn't about fixed positions or rigid roles. Instead, it emphasized fluidity, adaptability, and seamless interaction between players. To enact it successfully, each member of the team needed to read the situation, make quick decisions, and flow into the right position.

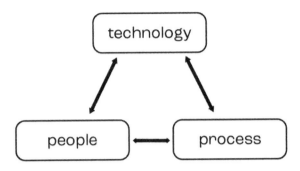

In the world of commercial real estate, we can apply a similar principle, in a system composed of three points: *process*, *people*, and *technology*. Instead of viewing these points as fixed pillars, we should see them as fluid, interconnected elements of our own "triangle offense." Like basketball players on the court, these elements need to work in harmony, constantly adjusting to the changing landscape of the market.

Let's break down each element of this CRE triangle offense.

Process: The Playbook

In basketball, the playbook defines how the team operates on the court. In CRE, your playbook is composed of the processes you have chosen. Those processes dictate how your organization manages and monitors all aspects of your digital strategy.

Without clear processes, you risk falling into a "no team situation." Imagine a basketball team with no playbook, where each player runs their own plays independently. Chaos, right? The same applies in

CRE when different parts of an organization operate their own systems in isolation.

One management company learned this lesson the hard way. Half of their client's 350,000-square-foot complex lost video surveillance because of a $40 network switch that no one knew about—because it was not documented anywhere, none of the current staff even knew it existed. This "ghost switch," purchased years ago by a temporary contractor, had become a critical but invisible part of the infrastructure. It was like having a key player on the court that no one recognized or knew how to work with. When it went down, the system was inoperable. (See appendix F for the full story about OpticWise's experience with this management company.)

The solution? Implement a comprehensive Data & Digital Infrastructure Audit (DDIA) across your entire portfolio. Think of the DDIA as your team's film study session: It helps you identify all the players on your court—every piece of hardware, software, and data source—so you can eliminate ghost systems and create a clear picture of your digital ecosystem.

Then, collect that information into documentation such as network maps, asset inventories, and systems interoperability charts. These documents form the basis of your playbook, removing vulnerabilities and surprises.

Many commercial real estate organizations have fragmented processes, especially through the course of property acquisitions or changes in management companies. Developing a playbook for implementing best practices—such as regular audits of your digital infrastructure, clear documentation procedures for all digital systems, and standardized processes around data for all your properties—goes a long way toward ensuring your CRE operations run smoothly, with no costly surprises.

People: The Team

In Coach Jackson's triangle offense, every player needed to understand not just their role but how it fit into the larger system. In basketball, the point guard isn't expected to dunk the ball every time; their role is knowing when to pass and whom to pass to. In the context of a data-driven CRE operation, this means creating a team where each member understands their role in the data ecosystem and knows when to collaborate with specialists.

That's why, as the US hockey team's coach Brooks taught us, you have to select players who fit your innovative system. But building this team isn't always easy. You don't just want to hire the most technically skilled individuals; being a data scientist or IT professional doesn't necessarily mean the person is right for your organization. You want to find people who fit your culture and can adapt to and thrive in your data-centric approach to commercial real estate.

A midsized CRE firm implemented a cross-functional data team—comprising a leasing agent, a data analyst, and a building engineer—to optimize its leasing process. The leasing agent provided insights on tenant preferences and market trends; the data analyst processed historical leasing data and market comparisons; and the building engineer contributed data on space utilization and maintenance costs. By understanding their roles in the data ecosystem and collaborating effectively, the team was able to develop a dynamic pricing model that increased occupancy rates by 6 percent and improved lease renewal rates by 17 percent.

You might face resistance from long-time employees who are comfortable with traditional methods. It's like trying to teach a veteran player a new offensive system. The solution? Show, don't tell. Demonstrate the value of data-driven decision-making through pilot projects that show tangible benefits, such as cost savings or increased tenant satisfaction. Then, implement training programs to upskill existing staff on data and digital concepts and associated tools.

With all employees, foster a culture of continuous learning and adaptation to new technologies and encourage cross-functional collaboration between traditional real estate roles and data-empowered roles. Most people become highly motivated when they understand their importance within the group and how their role contributes to the team's success.

Technology: The Equipment

In basketball, having the right shoes, the right ball, and the right training equipment can make all the difference. In a data-driven CRE organization, the right technology—not just software for data analysis, but also the underlying digital infrastructure that collects and transmits data—is essential to support both your processes and your people.

The flow of data is crucial in a data-driven operation. The data must be sent to or from a system independently to wherever the operator specifies it. This highlights the need for technologies that allow for both "push" and "pull" data-sharing capabilities (as introduced in chapter 2). For instance, a smart building system should be able to automatically log energy consumption data to a central database (push), while other operations systems respond to data inquiries (pull). It's like having a basketball that can magically pass itself to the open player.

However, many CRE organizations find themselves locked into vendor ecosystems that limit data access and control—like being forced to play ball with equipment that doesn't quite fit your style. The solution is simple: When negotiating with technology vendors, insist on data ownership and access rights. For example, your system needs to be pollable (pull) and should be able to log externally (push), not just internally to a vendor's database.

Looking at the big picture, be sure that your data-driven organization invests in scalable technologies that can grow with your portfolio. Prioritize systems that allow for data interoperability and easy integration, and implement robust cybersecurity measures to protect sensitive data. Using the right equipment is instrumental in building a championship-level CRE team.

OWN YOUR DAMN DATA!

As Vance and Vicki contemplated this CRE triangle offense, they realized that success wasn't about perfecting each element in isolation. It was about creating a system where process, people, and technology worked together fluidly, each enhancing the others. Like a well-oiled basketball team running the triangle offense, they needed every part of their organization to read the market, make quick decisions, and smoothly adapt to change. Furthermore, the team had to be able to rely on accurate, accessible data to inform its every move.

As Dave had pointed out, they weren't just in the real estate business anymore; they were in the data business. And in the modern commercial real estate landscape, data isn't just an asset—it's the lifeblood of your operation. There's a fundamental principle that can make or break your success in the data-driven era: *Own your damn data!*

And please, don't just take our word for it. A team of McKinsey analysts shared their research on data usage in the *Harvard Business Review* with a bold finding: "Companies that treat data like a product can reduce the time it takes to implement it in new use cases by as much as 90 percent, decrease their total ownership (technology, development, and maintenance) costs by up to 30 percent, and reduce their risk and data governance burden."[9]

Upholding data sovereignty—when you maintain autonomy and control over your data—is crucial to your success as a CRE operator. Data forms the foundation for all BI, AI, and advanced analytics, serving as the fuel that powers innovative solutions and competitive advantages. Without ownership and control of this vital resource, even the most sophisticated AI tools become ineffective.

The competitive advantages of data ownership in commercial real estate are manifold and significant. Consider the case of a property group that increased its net operating income by 4 percent by implementing data-driven pricing for its flexible office spaces. This was only possible because the group owned and could freely analyze their historical occupancy data, lease terms, and local market trends.

Similarly, predictive maintenance, powered by owned data from IoT sensors throughout properties and by manufacturers' recommended upkeep schedules, has revolutionized how real estate firms approach building upkeep. One firm slashed maintenance costs by 15 percent while simultaneously boosting tenant satisfaction scores. How did they achieve this? By predicting and preventing equipment failures before they occurred, all thanks to their owned sensor data.

Data ownership also paves the way for enhanced tenant retention strategies. By analyzing data on tenant behavior, usage patterns,

---

9   Veeral Desai, Tim Fountaine and Kayvaun Rowshankish, "A Better Way to Put Your Data to Work," *Harvard Business Review*, July–August 2022, https://hbr.org/2022/07/a-better-way-to-put-your-data-to-work.

and satisfaction surveys, property managers can proactively address issues and tailor services. One commercial property manager saw their tenant retention rate soar by nearly 9 percent after implementing such data-driven tenant engagement strategies.

Navigating Security and Privacy

However, with great data comes great responsibility. The legal and ethical considerations surrounding data ownership and use are complex and must be navigated correctly. Privacy regulations like GDPR and CCPA loom large in the data landscape. Collecting any personally identifiable information on tenants is a huge no-no, and responsible property owners should develop privacy statements that proudly state their policy against doing so. This approach not only ensures compliance but can also serve as a competitive advantage, positioning properties as not just outfitted with smart technology, but secure and respectful of user privacy.

Information security is a critical concern for any CRE property in the twenty-first century. It includes protection from unauthorized digital access or damage and can be broadly described as including the following:

- *Cybersecurity* specifically refers to protecting digital systems and networks from cyber threats or malicious intruders.

- *Data security* is a subset of cybersecurity focused solely on protecting data from unauthorized access, modification, or disclosure.

- *Identity management* refers to verifying who a user is before granting them access to sensitive information or systems, by managing and monitoring their digital identities.

Long-term information security success comes only from working with vendors, contractors, and consultants who prioritize data security and privacy to protect your newly unified digital infrastructure, its systems, and its users (see Figure 6). Yet, implementing robust security measures isn't just about protecting assets—it's about maintaining the trust of tenants and partners.

Figure 6. Information Security Measures

Encryption	**Antivirus Software**
Uses unique codes to scramble data so it's inaccessible to intruders.	Warns users of suspicious activity and takes action to protect data.
Access Control	**Application Security**
Determines who can access data and corporate resources.	Protects data from attackers by scanning for faults, threats, and credibility.
Firewalls	**Cloud Security**
Protects computers from hackers by allowing authorized connections and blocking unauthorized ones.	Protects cloud-based infrastructure, applications, and data.
Password Policy	**Authentication and Identity Management**
Ensures passwords are kept secret and don't change outside of the policy.	Ensuring that only authorized individuals can access specific resources.
Data Masking	**Information Privacy**
Helps protect whole data or specific data areas from exposure to unauthorized or malicious sources, whether externally or internally.	Involves safely handling the collection, storage, and distribution of information, including to third parties.

Jumping into the Data Lake

Whether you're a seasoned data expert or just starting your journey, you'll need to think long and hard about how to build a winning data strategy. You want to be sure you're choosing the right tools for optimizing your data architecture and leveraging your data for maximum impact. So, before designing and creating your data infrastructure, it's essential to understand the difference between **data lakes** and **data warehouses**.

Both alternatives store data, but they have different structures, objectives, and requirements. A data warehouse is a repository for structured data that are alike. In the context of commercial real estate, this might be your access control logs, with fields like *Who, What, When,* and *Where.* A data lake, on the other hand, is more comprehensive and flexible, consisting of multiple data warehouses and capable of storing structured, unstructured, or semi-structured data. This means a data lake can accommodate a wide variety of data types, from highly structured information to completely unstructured data.

In real estate, you can think of a data lake as a vast, digital property that houses all of your information. Just as a diverse real estate portfolio might include office buildings, apartments, and retail spaces, a data lake contains various data types. The structured data, like tenant lease information, is similar to a well-organized office building. Semi-structured data, such as maintenance logs, is more like a flexible co-working space. Unstructured data, like tenant communications, resembles a bustling community area where interactions happen freely.

To shift to a sports analogy: A data warehouse is like a structured baseball scorecard, filled in with specific stats by spectators as the game unfolds. Building a data lake, however, is like giving each spectator in the stadium a blank notepad to write down anything they notice about the ball game. The scorecard provides consistent, easily analyzable data. The notepads might capture unexpected insights beyond the structured scorecard but require more effort to analyze data systematically.

(For those eager to dive deeper into the world of data lakes, we've compiled a comprehensive guide in appendix D to help you take your data game to the next level.)

As Vance and Vicki contemplated all the considerations around data infrastructure and ownership, they remembered that crucial piece of advice: *If you're not monetizing your data, then someone else probably is.* Leaving this potential revenue stream untapped is like leaving money on the table. And leveraging their data would be possible only if they owned it—and could secure it. By taking ownership of their data and digital infrastructure while carefully navigating the security, legal, and ethical landscapes, they weren't just improving operational efficiency. They were positioning their organization to play on its home turf, with all the advantages that come with it.

HOME TEAM VERSUS VISITOR: NEGOTIATING ALLIANCES WITH VENDORS

In the complex, competitive world of commercial real estate, property owners often find themselves at a crossroads when dealing with vendors and their systems: Who will have control over the CRE owner's data—the vendor or the owner? It's akin to deciding whether you're playing on your home turf, which brings a sense of security and other advantages, or as a visitor in someone else's stadium. To ensure you maintain control of such a valuable asset, skillful negotiation is critical.

During negotiations, it's crucial to look beyond surface-level promises. When OpticWise clients ask about data ownership, often the vendor will say, "Sure, yeah, you can log in and see the data. It's yours, it's yours." Vendors may claim that the data is "yours," but what does that really mean in practice? Simply viewing the data is not enough; you need the ability to extract, analyze, and leverage it for your strategic decision-making. The data needs to be accessible and portable.

When negotiating with vendors, approach the conversation with a clear strategy and a thorough understanding of your needs. Your property is unique, and your vision for its future should drive the conversation. Don't let vendors dictate the direction with their prepackaged solutions. Articulating your goals and expectations will set the tone for the entire negotiation.

Also, be alert to potential conflicts of interest that could influence the vendor's recommendations. These negotiations are not just about getting the best price; they're about ensuring that the vendor's offerings align with your long-term goals, including those for data ownership and utilization.

To establish a partnership that truly serves your interests and supports your journey toward becoming a data-driven real estate dynasty, follow these five key steps in negotiations:

1. Ask the right questions upfront.

2. Look beyond surface-level promises.

3. Insist on data ownership, accessibility, and portability.

4. Set clear deadlines for meeting your requirements.

5. Aim for **bidirectional data flow** capabilities.

Asking a vendor the right questions from the outset is crucial. When you ask these questions, they must answer—but if you don't ask, they likely won't tell you. To help both your internal team and the vendor step back and consider the bigger picture, consider the following fundamental questions about alignment. The questions broadly fall into three categories: *vision*, *offerings*, and *ownership*.

1. Vision

   › How does your proposed solution specifically address our property's unique needs and long-term goals?

   › Can you demonstrate how your solution will add value beyond our current systems and processes?

   › Given your company's size, how do you ensure personalized attention and customization for each of our specific properties?

   › Who controls the **user experience**?

2. Offerings

   › What hardware components are included or required in your proposal? (Please provide a detailed breakdown.)

   › What software platforms are included in your proposal, and how can they connect to and with our existing systems?

   › Can you outline the full scope of services covered in this proposal, including implementation and ongoing support?

> Can you provide details on your performance monitoring processes, and how we'll be kept informed?

3. Ownership

> Do you or your company have any real estate holdings that compete with our property?

> Do you or your company have any financial interests or partnerships with the vendors or solutions you're recommending?

> Do you or your company stand to gain financially in some way if we sign a contract with any of your recommended vendors?

> How will we maintain ownership and control of our property's data throughout our partnership?

> What level of access and portability will we have to our data, both during and after our contract term?

> How does your solution allow connection with third-party systems, data repositories, or future technologies we might adopt?

> Does your solution require an isolated network? If so, why?

In our experience at OpticWise, these questions are essential to achieving the desired results in vendor negotiations.

For example, we once assisted a property owner using a system that specialized in co-working spaces. Initially, the vendor offered a closed system that was unable to connect to our client's digital infrastructure. Through our determined effort, however, the vendor ultimately agreed to update their system to include robust data-sharing capabilities. This involved two key phases—first, identifying specific data requirements and setting up basic sharing protocols, and second, building more comprehensive integrations through APIs and webhooks—and was a complex process. But when the property owner shared details via the questions outlined here, the vendor recognized the potential for alignment and bought into the owner's vision.

This negotiation process isn't always smooth sailing. Vendors may resist requests for greater data accessibility and control. In such cases, it's advisable to give them "time to cure"—essentially, a deadline to meet your data accessibility requirements. Offering two to four months to get the data flowing out of their system puts pressure on the vendors to adapt to your needs rather than the other way around.

Some vendors will refuse to buy in and won't participate unless it's on their terms. Fortunately, the same three categories of questions listed earlier will illuminate the need to find a different partner and solution.

Remember, too, that when it comes to choosing the right vendor for your organization, bigger doesn't always mean better. The size and perceived prestige of a company could actually be a net negative. "Bigs" often want to sell their packaged offerings, not custom solutions. Additionally, these organizations' time, attention, and focus may be limited due to the vast size of their operations. So don't get "wowed" by the size, marketing, and rhetoric of the bigs—kick the tires . . . hard. Use the vendor questions listed earlier to ensure your potential partner is using your data wisely and ethically to create real value for your organization.

The goal of your vendor negotiations should be to create a system that's both pollable (allowing you to retrieve data on demand) and pushable (automatically sending data to your central repository). Ideally, data movement would be both from their side and from your data infrastructure side. This bidirectional data flow is necessary if your CRE organization is to achieve real-time monitoring, comprehensive analytics, and the agility to respond quickly to changing conditions in your properties.

Among the many brilliant pieces of advice to be learned from entrepreneurial coach Dan Sullivan's many successful books, one standout is the same as the book's title: *Always Be the Buyer*.[10] Keep this in mind as you approach vendors and strive to negotiate the best possible deal for your company. Don't assume a seller's role, trying to promote yourself to the vendor. As the buyer, you hold the cards and make the decisions about whom to work with—don't give up that control.

By approaching vendor negotiations with clarity, persistence, and a firm understanding of your organization's data needs, you can transform from an average performer to a true dynastic champion in the competitive world of commercial real estate.

MOVING FROM CONTROL TO COORDINATION

Sitting down for their next meeting with the OpticWise consultants, Vance and Vicki expressed their sincere gratitude for Dave and Kaylie's patience. "We've decided not to work with MegaProp Solutions," Vance said.

---

10 Dan Sullivan, *Always Be the Buyer: Attracting Other People's Highest Commitment to Your Biggest and Best Standards* (Author Academy Elite, 2019).

Dave smiled. "That's a wise decision. Building the best team and offense isn't about outsourcing to the biggest name or relying on a property management group that claims technical prowess. It's about creating a data-driven culture within your own organization, where *you* are in the driver's seat."

Kayle nodded. "Now let's discuss how we can help you build that team and that strategic offense, starting from the top. It's time to coordinate your data sources into a focused strategy."

As Dave and Kaylie began outlining their vision for VRE's digital transformation, Vance and Vicki continued to thank their lucky stars. They had narrowly avoided a costly mistake. Now they were ready to truly build their best team—one that would turn their properties into champions while they maintained ownership and control of their valuable data and digital infrastructure.

CHAPTER 3 TAKEAWAYS

1. Cultivate a data-driven dynasty. Foster a culture that values and leverages data at every level of your organization, from the C-suite to maintenance staff.

2. Master the CRE triangle offense. Implement and balance the three key elements—process, people, and technology—to create a winning strategy for your real estate operations.

3. Own your data, own your future. Understand the critical importance of data ownership and maintain control over your digital infrastructure to drive competitive advantage.

4. Negotiate like a champion. Learn to strategically engage with vendors, achieving data ownership and access rights that benefit your organization over the long term.

5. Build your data lake. Construct and optimize a comprehensive data repository, transforming raw information into the basis for actionable insights that drive decision-making.

6. Navigate the data ethics landscape. Balance legal and ethical considerations in data management to build trust with tenants and partners while staying compliant.

7. Assemble your dream team. Recruit, train, and nurture a team that understands and values data-driven decision-making, fostering innovation across your organization.

8. Stay ahead of the game. Continuously adapt and refine your data strategy, embracing new technologies and methodologies to maintain your competitive edge in the dynamic real estate market.

TAKE ACTION

Use the *vision*, *offerings*, and *ownership* questions to evaluate your current and potential vendors. Start with your most critical technology service provider and document their answers. This crucial step will help ensure you achieve control of your data and digital infrastructure while building the right partnerships for your championship team.

CHAPTER 4

Coordinate: Preseason Training

"Talent wins games, but teamwork and
intelligence win championships."

—Michael Jordan, six-time NBA champion (Chicago Bulls)

FROM SINGLES TO DOUBLES,
TRIPLES, AND HOME RUNS

Vance and Vicki sat in their office, surrounded by charts, graphs, and data reports. The past few months had been a whirlwind of activity as they implemented the strategies suggested by Dave and Kaylie from OpticWise and began making sense of all the data they were collecting from their properties. It was truly hard work, but they were excited about the possibilities that lay ahead of them.

"We've come a long way, haven't we?" Vance said, picking up one report. "Who would have thought measuring actual water volume instead of total volume could make such a difference? I can't believe we were paying for the air bubbles, too."

Every time Vicki told this story, she could not hold back a smile.

"A thirty percent reduction in our water bill is something to celebrate. And Dave and Kaylie said this is just the tip of the iceberg."

Vance leaned back in his chair. "You're right. We've made headway in collecting most of our data, but it's still a work in progress. We're moving the needle. But where do we go from here?"

Vicki pulled out a folder labeled *Utility Optimization*. "Well, now that we've tackled water, I think it's time we look at our other utility options. Particularly, I'm interested in exploring how we can optimize our energy usage in common spaces."

Vance frowned. "That's a great idea, but I'm worried about Kevin." One of VRE's building engineers, Kevin, had seemed resistant toward new systems to monitor occupancy, heat, air, and gas usage, and correlate them with time-of-use, billing, and weather data.

As if on cue, a knock came at the door.

"Perfect timing," Vicki said, gesturing for Dave and Kaylie to enter and sit down. "We were just discussing our next steps."

Dave set his laptop on the table. "Great minds think alike. We've been analyzing your data, and we think there's a significant opportunity in optimizing your common area utilities."

Kaylie nodded, pulling up a presentation on her laptop. "Based on our calculations, we believe you could save at least ten percent on your overall utility costs by implementing some key changes. We've seen some properties save more than twenty percent."

Vance's eyes widened. "Ten percent? That's substantial when you consider our entire portfolio."

"Exactly," Dave said. "But here's the thing: We don't think Kevin, or any single building engineer, can handle this level of data analysis and AI implementation on their own."

Vicki and Vance exchanged glances.

"We were just discussing that," Vicki admitted. "We realize we might need additional skill sets."

"You're absolutely right," Kaylie agreed. "To truly leverage AI and maximize the return on your data, you need a team with specialized skills. We're talking data scientists, AI specialists, and people who can translate these insights into actionable strategies."

"But what about Kevin?" Vance asked, concern evident in his voice. "We value his expertise and experience."

Dave nodded understandingly. "Kevin's role is crucial. He knows these buildings inside and out. The idea isn't to replace him but to augment his capabilities. Once we have the AI-driven insights, we can work with Kevin to implement strategies and control these systems."

Kaylie nodded. "That sort of coordination is how we'll go from simply hitting singles to knocking the baseball out of the park."

Vance stood up and walked to the window, looking out at their downtown property. "It's a big step," he said, turning back to the group. "But I think it's necessary if we want to stay competitive and truly optimize our operations."

"I agree," Vicki said, showing the same moxie she'd been known for on the field during her college sports career. "We've seen what data can do with just our water systems. Imagine what we could achieve across our entire portfolio."

Dave had prepared for this moment and pulled out a detailed plan. "Yes, let's discuss how we can start coordinating these efforts. We've outlined a strategy that combines occupancy data, weather patterns, time-of-day usage, and your HVAC systems. It may seem complex, but the potential savings and efficiency gains are substantial."

As Dave and Kaylie began to explain their plan, Vance and Vicki listened intently, occasionally asking questions or providing insights about their properties. The office buzzed with energy as they delved into the details, all of them aware that they were on the cusp of a significant transformation in how Victors Real Estate Group managed their real estate portfolio.

"Alright," Vance said as the meeting wound down, "let's do this. It's time to take our data game to the next level. Where do we start?"

Kaylie grinned, pulling up a new slide on her laptop. "We thought you'd never ask. Let's begin with your downtown office building . . ."

Chapter 4 Goals

This chapter focuses on the Coordinate stage of the 5C process. You'll learn how to transform isolated data points into actionable intelligence by blending different data sources, much like a championship team combines various insights to make winning decisions. We'll explore working with data scientists and AI tools to uncover patterns, create predictive models, and develop algorithms that drive real value for your properties.

You'll learn to select and execute your first data-driven plays, balancing ambition with achievability. Whether you're building in-house capabilities, partnering with experts, or pursuing a hybrid approach, this chapter will equip you to make informed decisions about coordinating your data strategy. By the end, you'll understand how to address specific problems, from optimizing utilities to enhancing tenant experiences, and be prepared to scale your data strategy across your entire portfolio.

MAKING DATA MAKE SENSE: TWO WAYS TO SCORE

As Vance and Vicki embarked on their journey to leverage data and AI across their portfolio, they faced a fundamental question: How could they make sense of the vast amount of information at their disposal? The answer lies in understanding the difference between **single data sources** and **blended data** repositories, and how each can contribute to CRE operations and property management strategies.

Single Data Source

A single data source in commercial real estate refers to information collected from one specific system or component within a property. This can include data from lighting systems, HVAC controls, wireless access points, individual IoT sensors, and so forth. Leveraging single data sources allows CRE owners and operators to optimize individual systems, potentially leading to cost savings, improved efficiency, and better tenant experiences.

CRE organizations like Victors Real Estate appreciate the immediate wins in cost reduction and efficiency that come from relatively simple implementation and management of these data-driven changes. The long-term gains in improved performance of individual building components are enough to outweigh the challenges for some property owners, which can include the inconvenience of data siloed in disparate systems and the inability to run AI across multiple systems. But if your vendor partners are structured to retain control of their system's functionality and data access, which is often the case, you may wish to pursue a more advantageous option for coordinating your data.

Blended Data

Blended data involves the use of information from multiple systems or data sources within a property. This approach allows CRE owners and operators to uncover complex patterns, correlations, and insights that aren't apparent when looking at systems in isolation (i.e., single data source). Blended data analysis often requires more sophisticated tools, including AI and machine learning, to fully leverage the data's potential.

Adopting a blended data approach requires the CRE organization to use a data repository such as a data lake (discussed in chapter 3) and depends on analytics tools and AI to draw valuable insights. You also need to enlist vendors to cooperate in sharing data. This approach may even require strategic and skill set changes within your organization.

However, the benefits of using blended data are irresistible for many CRE owners and operators. Making data-driven decisions that consider the property holistically, and optimizing operations simultaneously across multiple systems, allows you to uncover hidden income opportunities. And the eye-opening advantages of predictive maintenance and proactive problem-solving not only make for more efficient operations but also create unique value propositions for your tenants.

As Vance and Vicki considered their next steps, they weighed the benefits and challenges of both single and blended data approaches. Their success, they realized, will depend on how effectively they coordinate these data sources to drive meaningful improvements across their portfolio.

GOOD SPORTS: Pedaling Toward Perfection[11]

The transformation of British Cycling—the UK's national governing body for cycle sport—under Dave Brailsford's leadership offers a powerful lesson for commercial real estate leaders on the potential of leveraging comprehensive data sources.

In 2003, British Cycling was a perennial underachiever, having won only a single gold medal in its seventy-six-year Olympic history. The team's performance was so poor that a leading bike manufacturer refused to sell them equipment, fearing it would hurt their brand. Enter Dave Brailsford with his revolutionary philosophy, based on what he called "the aggregation of marginal gains."

Brailsford's approach was simple yet profound: Improve every aspect of cycling by 1 percent, and the cumulative effect would be extraordinary. His team scrutinized everything from bike seat design to the type of massage gel used for muscle recovery. They painted the inside of the team truck white to spot dust that could degrade bike performance. They even researched the best pillows and mattresses to ensure each rider got the best possible night's sleep.

The results were staggering. Just five years later, at the 2008 Beijing Olympics, British cyclists won 60 percent of the possible gold medals for cycling. They continued this dominance in subsequent Olympics and Tour de France races, marking one of the most dramatic turnarounds in sports history.

The impact of Brailsford's marginal gains philosophy is evident in the team's results. By focusing on numerous small improvements across all aspects of the sport, British Cycling achieved an impressive

---

11   Matt Slater, "Olympics Cycling: Marginal Gains Underpin Team GB Dominance," BBC Sport, August 8, 2012, https://www.bbc.com/sport/olympics/19174302; Eben Harrell, "How 1% Performance Improvements Led to Olympic Gold," *Harvard Business Review*, October 30, 2015, https://hbr.org/2015/10/how-1-performance-improvements-led-to-olympic-gold; James Clear, "This Coach Improved Every Tiny Thing by 1 Percent and Here's What Happened" (blog post), https://jamesclear.com/marginal-gains; Shawn Callahan, "The Real Secret to British Cycling's Success: More Than Just Marginal Gains," Anecdote.com, July 1, 2024.

continued

performance record and remarkable success. This transformation parallels the potential in commercial real estate when examining data from all systems, considering it from a holistic viewpoint. CRE organizations can achieve significant gains by leveraging comprehensive data sources, which reveals potential improvements that might not be apparent when looking at systems in isolation.

Just as British Cycling sought 1 percent improvements in various areas, your CRE company can focus on small, incremental enhancements across multiple systems. These might include minor adjustments to HVAC settings, slight modifications to lighting schedules, or small changes in space utilization. While each improvement might seem small on its own, the cumulative effect can be substantial, leading to significant synergies and overall improvements in efficiency, tenant satisfaction, and property value. Importantly, Brailsford's approach recognized that data-driven improvement came not from a one-time overhaul but from ongoing data analysis to constantly refine and optimize building performance.

British Cycling went from nearly zero to hero in just five years. With the right data strategy, your properties could experience a similarly dramatic leap in performance and value. The future of CRE belongs to those who can leverage comprehensive data to drive continuous improvement. Are you ready to pedal toward perfection?

Key Takeaways for Real Estate

Like athletes on the British Cycling team, successful real estate operators need to:

- Consider data from and across all systems to gain a comprehensive view of each property's performance.
- Focus on making incremental modifications and improvements across multiple areas.
- Be patient as minor individual improvements accumulate for a transformative effect.
- Embrace a culture of continuous, data-driven optimization.

PLAYING WITH THE POSSIBILITIES OF YOUR DATA

As Vance and Vicki discovered in their journey, the transformation of British Cycling offers a compelling parallel for the potential of comprehensive data analysis in commercial real estate. Just as Dave Brailsford's cycling team found marginal gains in every aspect of the sport, property owners and operators can uncover significant improvements across their portfolios by leveraging both single data sources and blended data. Diving into this ocean of possibilities will reveal countless innovations that you can bring to your CRE game.

The possibilities for improvement, innovation, and growth lie in the intelligent use of these data types. Single data sources, such as those from individual systems like HVAC or lighting, offer quick wins and efficiency gains. However, the real magic happens when we blend data from multiple sources, allowing us to see the bigger picture and uncover hidden correlations and opportunities.

Collaborating with a data scientist or expert consultants to support your work is like having a high-performance coach for your properties. These experts excel at identifying patterns and trends across blended datasets, revealing insights that might otherwise go unnoticed. Their skills can lead to substantial performance enhancements across your portfolio.

Armed with advanced algorithms and data models, data experts can forecast outcomes with unprecedented accuracy. This predictive capability allows CRE operators to anticipate maintenance needs *before* equipment fails and to project energy consumption based on factors like weather patterns and occupancy trends. We're not just analyzing current conditions; we're peering into the future of property and operations management by combining data from and across various sources.

Artificial intelligence takes this a step further, continuously refining our data quality, uncovering efficiency gains, and improving offerings to tenants. The key is translating these insights from blended data sources into tangible operational improvements. This requires clear communication of recommendations to teams and executives, using data visualization tools that make complex information easily digestible.

Modern data science allows us to consolidate information from diverse sources into a single repository, moving beyond the limitations of single data sources. When coupled with machine learning, this comprehensive view enables more informed decision-making, helping us understand how all aspects of a property interact.

Many CRE operators want to take it a step further, using business intelligence (BI). This obtainable goal starts with data at the core, then applies AI—specifically, machine learning—to create actionable insights. (For more about AI and BI, see appendix C.) Think of this as creating a rulebook for a modern AI system that works tirelessly, making decisions based on a breadth of information no single human could process. This approach ensures that critical knowledge remains with your organization, even as personnel changes occur—a concern Vance and Vicki had regarding their building engineer, Kevin.

Consider a Formula One racing team. During a race, they use real-time data from multiple sources to make split-second decisions about tire changes, refueling, and strategy adjustments. Similarly, an AI system for your properties can continuously monitor performance metrics like energy usage, occupancy patterns, and maintenance needs, making automatic adjustments to optimize operations. Just as a racing team adapts to changing track conditions, your properties can respond to fluctuations in tenant needs, weather, or energy prices by leveraging blended data insights.

The potential of a data-driven approach is not just vast—it's transformative. As PwC has stated, "AI could contribute up to $15.7 trillion to the global economy in 2030, more than the current output of China and India combined. Of this, $6.6 trillion is likely to come from increased productivity and $9.1 trillion is likely to come from consumption-side effects."[12] Choosing a data-driven approach elevates operations managers from mere overseers to strategic performance optimizers, capable of enhancing efficiency and value across entire portfolios. By embracing the power of blended data, we unlock a world of unprecedented insights and improvements in commercial real estate management.

To truly grasp the revolutionary potential that awaits, let's explore a selection of *What if?* scenarios—more than fifty possible strategies to help you hit a home run for your organization.

FIFTY-FIVE WAYS TO WIN: PATHWAYS TO PEAK PERFORMANCE

The following list of blended data scenarios offers a chance for CRE owners and operators to think beyond the obvious. Leverage these suggestions with your own ingenuity—the sky's the limit on possible

---

12 PwC, "Sizing the Prize: What's the Real Value of AI for Your Business and How Can You Capitalise?" (2017), https://www.pwc.com/gx/en/issues/analytics/assets/pwc-ai-analysis-sizing-the-prize-report.pdf.

combinations and upside. How might these ideas apply to your specific properties? What unique combinations could you create for using your data to the fullest? Remember, in the world of data-driven real estate management, the only limit is our imagination.

These thought provokers and starting ideas will help deliver your slice of that massive, multitrillion-dollar pie. Each scenario presented here is a hypothesis. Some of these are tried and tested solutions. Others are strong ideas based on our experience and knowledge. It's important to remember that working with data and digital infrastructures is both an art and a science, as we explain in chapter 5. We must run the experiments in pursuit of peak performance.

To navigate these exciting, almost endless possibilities, consider examples from each of the six key data and digital infrastructure domains (introduced in chapter 1), with the recommended systems in boldface followed by the potential results of this blended data approach.

Network Infrastructure and IoT

- **Tenant communication platforms + WiFi usage data** = personalized digital experiences as tenants move through the building, enhancing the perceived value of your amenities.

- **Internet circuit performance data + business intelligence platforms** = optimal connectivity for tenants, reducing churn and attracting tech-savvy tenants.

- **Voice services + natural language processing + building control systems** = voice-controlled smart building interfaces that can differentiate the property in a competitive market.

- **Asset tracking systems + room scheduling** = optimized placement and utilization of movable assets (e.g., projectors, whiteboards), reducing equipment purchases.

- **Temperature and humidity sensors + tenant feedback systems** = personalized comfort zones for different tenants, increasing tenant satisfaction and retention rates.

- **Asset tracking systems + 3D building information modeling + augmented reality** = a visual system for locating and maintaining building capital assets, reducing time spent on maintenance tasks.

- **Network security data + access control systems** = more secure and reliable connected environments, reducing security and cybersecurity risks.

Security, Access Control, and Risk Management

- **Occupancy sensors + smart locks + AI** = intelligent security systems that automatically secure unused areas, reducing security personnel costs.

- **Keys management + access control systems + tenant management** = comprehensive digital access systems that reduce administrative costs while improving security.

- **Access control systems + after-hours detection** = enhanced security during off-hours plus reduced energy usage that improves building efficiency.

- **Emergency response systems + building layout data** = optimized emergency protocols and response times, improving safety protocols and outcomes.

- **Security monitoring** + **advanced analytics** = identification of behavior patterns and potential issues before they become problems, preventing security incidents.

- **Surveillance data** + **lighting controls** = enhanced security alongside reduced energy costs in low-traffic areas during off-hours.

- **Leak detection** + **historical water usage patterns** + **predictive maintenance** = identification of potential water system failures, avoiding costly water damage and disruptions.

- **Video recording** + **intrusion detection** = reduced false alarms and security personnel costs while improving overall security.

Energy, Environmental Management, and Sustainability

- **Smart thermostats** + **weather forecast data** + **occupancy patterns** = predictive HVAC systems that optimize operations, reducing energy costs while maintaining tenant comfort.

- **Occupancy sensors** + **lighting systems** + **natural light sensors** = intelligent lighting that balances artificial and natural light, optimizing energy efficiency while improving occupant comfort.

- **Large motors usage** + **power quality monitoring** + **time-of-use billing rules** = more effective management of startup load spikes and reduced peak loads, reducing overall energy costs.

- **Green building certification management** + **energy simulation tools** = identification of the most cost-effective sustainability upgrades, maximizing ROI on green investments.

- **Air quality monitors + HVAC systems + weather forecast data** = optimized indoor air quality and energy usage, improving tenant health and satisfaction.

- **Waste management systems + supply chain data** = closed-loop waste management systems that reduce disposal costs while generating new revenue streams.

- **Utility usage data + AI-powered analytics** = identification of consumption patterns and optimization opportunities, reducing overall utility costs.

- **Building certification data + performance metrics** = tracked and improved sustainability ratings, which increases property value.

- **Submetering (electric and gas) + time-of-use utility rates + energy management systems** = energy-intensive activities shifted to off-peak hours, reducing overall energy costs.

- **Solar systems + energy management + weather forecast data** = optimized renewable energy usage, maximizing cost savings and sustainability benefits.

- **Utility water systems data + weather forecast data** = optimized irrigation schedules for landscaping, reducing water consumption and associated costs.

- **Solar systems performance + EV charging usage** = maximized use of renewable energy for EV charging, offering green charging as a premium service.

- **Environmental compliance monitoring + energy management + predictive analytics** = a system that automatically adjusts building operations to stay within compliance thresholds, avoiding fines.

Property Operations and Tenant Experience

- **Facilities management data + predictive maintenance systems** = ability to address issues before tenants notice them, improving satisfaction while reducing emergency repair costs.
- **Amenity booking systems + usage analytics** = optimized amenity offerings and availability, increasing their value to tenants.
- **Event space data + community engagement tools** = optimized event space usage and programming, increasing revenue from bookings.
- **Concierge services + occupancy analytics + tenant communication platforms** = personalized, location-based services offered to tenants, creating new revenue streams.
- **Parking management + local event data + dynamic pricing algorithms** = optimized parking revenue based on demand patterns, maximizing income from parking assets.
- **Cleaning schedules + occupancy data** = optimized maintenance timing and resources, reducing costs while improving cleanliness.
- **Air quality data + wellness metrics** = creating and marketing of premium, healthy spaces, justifying the higher rents.

- **Tenant communication tools + service request data** = improved response times and satisfaction, reducing tenant turnover.

- **Noise level sensors + space utilization data** = more effective noise reduction strategies in high-traffic areas, increasing their usability and value.

- **Room scheduling + indoor air quality management + HVAC optimization** = pre-conditioned meeting rooms based on expected occupancy, optimizing energy use while ensuring comfort.

- **Facilities management + expense tracking** = identification and application of optimal cost-effective maintenance strategies, reducing overall OpEx.

Financial and Asset Management

- **Operational cost data + performance analytics** = cost-saving opportunities identified and implemented, improving NOI across the portfolio.

- **Capital planning tools + building performance data** = optimized improvement schedules and budgets, maximizing ROI on capital investments.

- **Real-time asset performance + historical data** = more accurate performance forecasts that improve budget accuracy.

- **Vendor contract data + service performance metrics** = optimized service agreements and costs, reducing operating expenses.

- **Space utilization + revenue analytics** = dynamic pricing strategies that maximize revenue per square foot.

- **Insurance analytics + predictive maintenance + risk management data** = proactive risk management demonstrated to insurers, reducing insurance premiums.

- **Operational metrics + financial planning tools** = more accurate budgets and forecasts, improving financial planning accuracy.

- **Benchmarking tools + investment performance analytics** = identification of underperforming assets and prioritization of capital improvements for maximum ROI.

- **Asset tracking systems + predictive maintenance scheduling + capital equipment usage data** = a comprehensive asset lifecycle management system that extends equipment life, optimizes equipment maintenance schedules, and improves asset longevity while reducing replacement costs.

- **Business intelligence platforms + property management data** = identification of trends in maintenance requests, for proactive handling of common issues and reduced overall maintenance costs.

Data Aggregation and Analytics

- **Maintenance records + AI-powered analytics** = identification of patterns and predictions on future needs, reducing unexpected repairs and costs.

- **Market data + property performance metrics + predictive** analytics = the ability to forecast trends and adapt pricing dynamically and proactively, staying ahead of market changes.

- **Occupancy analytics + space utilization data** = optimized floor plans and space usage, increasing rentable square footage and revenue.

- **Retail analytics + foot traffic data** = valuable insights into retail tenants, increasing their success and, ultimately, tenant retention.

- **Portfolio performance data + industry benchmarks** = identification of opportunities for improvements that can optimize returns across properties.

- **Operational data from multiple properties** = identification of best practices and inefficiencies, improving portfolio-wide performance.

This extensive array of potential data combinations should spark your imagination and illustrate the boundless opportunities that emerge when you blend different data sources for a holistic big-picture perspective that will significantly improve your real estate game.

Yet Vance and Vicki's excitement about these possibilities is just beginning.

SELECTING THE INITIAL THREE PLAYS FOR YOUR PLAYBOOK

Blended data offers a vast landscape of possibilities that can be exhilarating but also overwhelming. As Vance and Vicki soon realized, the key to success lies not in trying to implement everything at once, but in strategically selecting your first moves. When adding these initial plays to your playbook, it's crucial to align them with metrics that support your overall vision. So, let's take a breath, focus, and break down the process of selecting these initial plays that will start you on the path to data-driven success.

Identify the Needle Movers

First, look for opportunities that can significantly impact your CRE operation. Which choices promise to be "needle movers" for your business, capable of dramatically improving overall property performance? The answer will vary depending on your specific goals, but they often fall into one of these outcome-based categories:

- **Tenant (occupant, guest, resident, etc.) experience:** These plays promise to dramatically enhance satisfaction and engagement.

- **Net operating income:** These initiatives can substantially increase revenue or decrease costs (or both).

- **Competitive advantage:** These are strategies that will set your properties apart in the marketplace.

For example, Vance and Vicki chose to focus initially on utility optimization, which promised to impact both their NOI and their competitive position by reducing costs and showcasing their commitment to sustainability while improving their pricing.

Ensure the Plays Are Achievable

While it's tempting to aim for the stars, it's crucial to start with plays that are within reach. You don't want to commit to climbing Mount Everest when you've never even tried a short hike. Look for opportunities that:

- Can be implemented with your current resources or with minimal additional investment.
- Have a clear path to implementation.
- Rely on data you already have or can easily acquire.
- Can show results in a reasonable time frame.

Remember, early wins build momentum and support for your data-driven initiatives.

Prioritize Learning Opportunities

Your initial plays should also serve as a learning experience. Consider selecting at least one play that:

- Allows you to experiment with a new type of data or analytics tool,
- Helps you establish baseline data for future initiatives, and/or
- Gives your team experience in working with data-driven decision-making.

When you take this approach, even a play that doesn't yield immediate financial results will still provide valuable insights and skills for future efforts.

As you evaluate potential plays for impact, achievability, and learning opportunities, consider creating a simple scoring system based on these three criteria. This can help you objectively compare different options and make informed decisions.

Vance and Vicki's journey provides a good example of this process in action. They started with utilities optimization, a play that promised significant cost savings (needle mover), could be implemented using data they already had access to (achievable), and offered them insight into data flow and analysis (learning opportunity). With that initial success under their belts, they prepared to move into areas like insurance reduction, a play that builds on their newfound data capabilities while tackling another major expense category.

Remember, the goal isn't to transform your entire operation overnight. Starting slow will allow you to continually improve and innovate as you build a data-driven culture and infrastructure. By carefully selecting your first three plays, you set the stage for long-term success in leveraging data to optimize your real estate portfolio.

EXECUTING YOUR PLAYBOOK

Now that you've added three plays to your playbook, it's time to move from strategy to execution. This transition is critical—it's where your data-driven vision begins to take tangible form. Having a clear action plan for implementation is just as important as choosing the right initiatives.

The first step in executing your playbook is to determine what you want your AI and BI initiatives to achieve. This involves defining your goals and exploring the market to see what solutions are available and at what cost.

Choosing an Approach: Build, Buy, or Hybrid?

Is it better to build your capabilities in-house, buy them from a vendor, or pursue a hybrid approach? The answer depends on you and your CRE organization.

Building your own data management system involves hiring data scientists and implementing an AI platform to run your data. This approach offers the most control and customization but requires significant investment in talent and technology. Building from the bottom up means you'd have to hire data experts and construct the platform to run the algorithms and host the data.

Buying this service, by partnering with a vendor that handles all aspects of data management and analysis, can be an attractive option. These firms often promise to cover two of the five *C*'s for you—Collect and Coordinate, but not Clarify, Connect, or Control. To cover all of the 5C Framework, you may have to engage multiple partners. And be sure to consider the scalability of this approach: You should be thinking about multiple properties, including those you have today and those you hope to build or acquire in the future.

A *hybrid* approach is the middle ground. It might involve hiring a data scientist to interface with a vendor that manages digital infrastructures and/or data acquisition and maintains your data lake, or vice versa. The hybrid model allows you to maintain some in-house expertise while leveraging external resources for more specialized or resource-intensive tasks.

A Note on Scale

As you consider these options, it's essential to think about scale. Your strategy needs to work not just for one building, but for your entire portfolio—both current and future. Whether you have five properties or five hundred, your approach needs to be scalable.

Cloud-based platforms offer the advantage of scaling as needed, which can be particularly attractive for CRE owners and operators with a growing portfolio. However, while big cloud-based companies excel at helping you build a data lake, they primarily help in the Coordinate area and may not be as effective in addressing all of the five *C*'s in the 5C Framework.

Similarly, big consulting firms can help you with Clarify and possibly Coordinate, but may not provide comprehensive solutions across other areas such as Connect or Control.

Making a Plan

Once you've decided on your approach, it's time to develop a detailed project plan. This comprehensive plan serves as your roadmap for execution, ensuring you fully understand and articulate the team's collective role, the resources available, and the expected outcomes. Designing your execution at this level of detail helps prevent misunderstandings and keeps the project on track. This plan should include the following:

- *Objective.* Clearly state what you aim to achieve with this initiative. Your objective should be SMART: specific, measurable, achievable, relevant, and time-bound.

- *Players/stakeholders.* Identify all parties involved, from internal team members to external partners, so everyone understands their role and responsibilities in working toward the project's success.

- *Digital and physical infrastructures.* Outline the technological and physical resources needed, from hardware and software to networks and any physical modifications required to your properties.

- *Data input.* Specify the data sources you'll be using. This could include existing systems, new sensors, external data sources, or a combination of these.

- *Data output.* Define the insights or actions you expect to generate from each initial play. Be clear about what success looks like in terms of the information or capabilities you'll gain.

- *AI tools and prompting.* Detail the AI tools you'll use and your initial hypotheses—the specific AI platforms or algorithms you plan to employ, and what you expect them to reveal or achieve.

- *Timeline/go live.* Set clear deadlines for each phase of the project. A well-defined timeline keeps the project on track and helps manage expectations.

- *Budget.* Allocate resources for each aspect of the initiative. Be sure to include both upfront costs and ongoing operating expenses.

- *R&R/accountability matrix.* Clearly define *roles, responsibilities,* and *accountability* for all involved parties. This matrix ensures that every aspect of the project has a designated owner and that all contributors understand their commitments.

For an example of how these initial moves might play out with your project or property, see our model plan (based on a real OpticWise engagement) in appendix G.

Remember, executing your playbook is an iterative process. Start with a solid plan, but remain flexible. Be prepared to adjust your approach based on early results and lessons learned. Keep your long-term vision in mind, however, as you navigate the exciting world of data-driven real estate operations and management.

FROM PRACTICE TO PERFORMANCE

As twilight settled over the city, Dave and Kaylie wrapped up this phase of work at VRE with Vance and Vicki. The office whiteboard that had once displayed basic property metrics now showcased complex data flows and AI implementation strategies.

"I have to admit," Vance said, studying their newly drafted project plan, "when we first started talking about blending different types of data, it seemed as daunting as learning a whole new sport. But breaking it down into these first three plays feels like we're building up to the championship rather than trying to win it all in one day."

Vicki nodded. "It reminds me of how we used to prepare for big games. You don't win championships by trying to master every play at once. You start with your fundamentals, perfect them, and then build your playbook from there."

"Exactly," Dave agreed. "And just like in sports, success comes from smart preparation and coordinated execution. You've already taken the first steps by identifying your initial focus areas. Now it's about bringing together your team, your technology, and your data to execute these plays."

"Speaking of execution," Kaylie added, pulling up a final slide, "your utility data analysis is already showing promising patterns.

Imagine what we'll discover once we start applying AI to all the data streams we've identified."

Vance and Vicki looked at their new partners knowingly, understanding that they were on the verge of transforming their operation from using simple data points to leveraging comprehensive, AI-driven insights. The possibilities seemed endless—from optimizing energy usage to predicting maintenance needs before they became a problem.

"You know what excites me most?" Vicki said, tapping her pen against the project timeline they'd just created. "This isn't just about making our current properties more efficient. We're building a foundation that will scale across our entire portfolio—present and future."

Vance nodded, thinking about how far they'd come since their first meeting with Dave and Kaylie. "A few months ago, I wouldn't have believed we could be talking about using AI to optimize our properties. Now it feels like we're just scratching the surface."

"Yes, you are," Dave smiled. "Think of this as your preseason training. You've got your playbook, you've selected your starting lineup of initiatives, and you've practiced the fundamentals. Now you're ready to put it all together and take it to the next level. It's time for the big game!"

The preseason was over; it was time to show what their properties could really do. Vance and Vicki were eager to transform their data coordination into countless victories. The Victors were finally ready to live up to their company's name.

CHAPTER 4 TAKEAWAYS

1. Understand data types. Learn the difference between single and blended data sources and how each contributes to property optimization.

2. Start small, think big. Select three initial plays that balance impact, achievability, and learning opportunities.

3. Plan thoroughly. Develop comprehensive project plans that address all aspects of implementation, from infrastructure to accountability.

4. Choose your approach. Decide whether to build in-house capabilities, buy solutions, or pursue a hybrid strategy based on your specific needs.

5. Think scalable. Ensure your data and AI strategy can grow with your portfolio.

6. Consider infrastructure needs. Account for both digital and physical infrastructure requirements in your planning.

7. Stay focused. Keep your strategic goals in mind while remaining flexible enough to adapt to new insights.

TAKE ACTION

Select your first three plays from the fifty-five ways to win, using the criteria—needle mover, achievability, and learning opportunity—outlined in this chapter. Document your selections and develop an initial hypothesis for each. This vital step will launch your journey from data collection to active coordination of your digital strategy.

CHAPTER 5

Control: It's Game Time

*"Think. Innovate. Find solutions. By your talent
and effort, you will be known."*

—**Jim Harbaugh,** NFL quarterback and coach, and NCAA
football championship coach (University of Michigan Wolverines)

CALLING BIG PLAYS

Vance and Vicki stood in their newly established operations center, a stark contrast to their old conference room. Wall-mounted displays showed real-time data streams from their portfolio—occupancy patterns, energy usage, maintenance alerts, and more. After months of running experimental plays, their business had transformed. Victors Real Estate Group had moved from basic analytics to active management.

"These utility savings have been solid," Vance said, studying a dashboard showing their portfolio-wide metrics, "but we're still just running safe plays up the middle. Where are our opportunities for some game-changing calls?"

Dave and Kaylie of OpticWise soon joined them at the VRE

command center for their weekly strategy session. The room hummed with the energy of a team ready to execute bigger plays.

"If you want to talk about game changers," Dave said, pulling up their operational analysis on the main screen, "let's look at your three biggest cost centers: utilities, vacancies, and insurance. You've made progress with utilities, but now it's time to take control of these other two opportunities."

An alert flashed on one of the screens—unusual occupancy patterns on floor 12. The system automatically adjusted the HVAC settings, but Vicki frowned.

"That's the kind of basic response we've mastered," she acknowledged. "But what about the bigger picture?"

"Like a quarterback reading the defense," Kaylie replied, "you'll learn to recognize where the big gains are possible. What's your current game plan for vacancies and insurance?"

"Finding new tenants is like having to keep recruiting new players—expensive and time-consuming," Vicki admitted.

"And with insurance," Vance added, "we're basically letting the underwriter control the game. Our premiums keep rising significantly, and we just accept it."

Dave held up his hand. "I think we can dramatically expand the playbook," he said. "Let's start with insurance—have you ever sat down with your underwriter to discuss what actions you could take to help lower your rates?"

Vance shook his head. "No, we usually just take whatever renewal quote they give us."

Kaylie picked up the topic. "Many underwriters will work with you on the quotes if you can show them you've got strong detection systems and clear response protocols, especially for things like water damage. It's about proving you have control and can limit certain risks on your properties." She explained that some property owners with a history of water-related events saw significant reductions—10 percent, as a conservative estimate—in premiums and deductibles.

Dave gestured at the screens. "Look at how far you've come. You clarified your assets—every system is mapped. You connected your digital infrastructure into one team. You collected your data and coordinated operations."

"And now comes the championship play: control," Kaylie added.

"Think of it like a quarterback in the Super Bowl," Dave continued. "That radio in his helmet? That's his direct line to execute the perfect play. You need the same thing—clear communication channels to your systems. When you call for an adjustment, your building needs to respond. When you spot a threat, your systems need to react. Without that command capability, you're like a coach trying to communicate with a QB who has a dead radio."

Vicki pointed to another alert flashing on the screen. "So instead of just basic responses like adjusting the HVAC, we need our systems to think ahead—like a quarterback reading the defense pre-snap?"

"Exactly," Kaylie nodded. "Your buildings need to anticipate and prepare for changing situations, not just react to them. We're going to help you communicate with your buildings in a way that gives you true control and makes all of your properties perform at peak levels."

The real game was just beginning, but Vance and Vicki were ready. They had developed a strong playbook. They had done enough film study and practice drills. Now it was time to take command of the game and blow the competition out of the water.

Chapter 5 Goals

This chapter will guide you through the critical transition from analysis to sustained action in your property operations. To win games, a championship team needs more than just a good scouting report—and you'll learn how to transform your CRE data insights into peak performance through effective system management, or Control—the fifth C in the 5C Framework.

You'll discover how to speak the language of your operating systems, ensuring your strategic decisions translate into real-world actions. We'll show you how to monitor data flows and system performance in real time, make adjustments when needed, and track progress through clear metrics. Like a quarterback with a radio in his helmet, you'll learn how to communicate precise commands to your systems and verify that they're being executed properly.

Most important, you'll learn how to build transparency and collaboration across your team, ensuring everyone understands their role in executing your data strategy. By the chapter's end, you'll have the tools and knowledge to take control of your property operations with championship-level precision, turning your analytical insights into winning results.

CONTROL THROUGH COMMUNICATION

In the previous chapter, we focused on **output data**—collecting and analyzing information from your property's systems. But championship teams don't win by observation alone. They win by executing smarter plays. Now it's time to master **input commands**—the key to control.

Many commercial properties are like a football team where each player can only see and act in response to their small part of the game: The HVAC system is like a lineman focused on the trenches. Access controls are like defensive backs watching their zones.

Lighting systems are like receivers running their routes. Each system speaks its own language and operates in its own sphere. Without coordination, you've got eleven players running different plays, for both offense and defense.

Football solved this communication problem with technology. Putting speakers in quarterbacks' helmets lets coaches in the skybox, who see the whole field, communicate directly with their quarterback, who then orchestrates the entire team's actions. Property owners need the same capability—a way to translate strategic vision into coordinated action across every system in your building.

But here's the challenge: This capability doesn't come standard. Many systems are like players who can only signal to the sideline but can't receive plays. They may collect and report data all day long, but they resist accepting commands from outside their own interfaces. This limitation cripples your ability to execute based on your insights.

That's why asking those questions about *vision, offerings,* and *ownership* (covered in chapter 3) before hiring any vendors is essential. Similarly, and before adding any system to your team roster, ask:

- Does the system accept external commands?
- What communication protocols does it use?
- How quickly can it respond?
- What security measures are in place?
- Can commands be automated?

The goal is bidirectional communication—systems that both report and respond. Think of it this way: Your occupancy sensors might spot an opportunity, like a defense system indicating a weakness. But if you can't call an audible—if you can't tell your HVAC to adjust or your lighting controls to modify—you're like a coach who sees the smarter strategic move but has no way to send in the play.

This matters more each day, as properties become increasingly integrated. Modern buildings need their systems to communicate with each other, like players adjusting to each other's movements on the field.

In a perfect world, however, they do not just need to communicate with each other—they need to communicate with your central business intelligence system. A central BI system is based on the data from your digital infrastructure, which is analyzed by your AI and your team. One system's insights should trigger responses from others. This orchestration only happens with clear command and control capabilities.

Don't settle for one-way communication (and certainly not for a total lack of communication). Your property's systems need to both listen and talk—just like a championship team must execute predetermined plays but also recognize unexpected opportunities. Output gives you the game film. Input gives you the win.

Even if you don't implement your own BI system, your team can translate the AI determinations and input them as controls and commands in each of your applicable operating systems. Some campuses warrant a centralized system, and some do not. Either way, you should utilize AI across disparate data sources to identify and implement optimizations wherever available.

Remember, just watching the game doesn't bring home trophies. Making the plays does. The same applies to your property. Collecting data is just the start. The ability to *act* on that data—through clear system communication—is what delivers championships.

GOOD SPORTS: It Don't Mean a Thing if it Ain't Got that Swing

Coach Al Ulbrickson had a vision: His 1936 University of Washington rowing team would achieve complete control. It would require relentless experimentation, but the results would be flawless.

In rowing, they call it "swing"—that magical moment when eight individual rowers become one unified force. Daniel James Brown's *The Boys in the Boat* describes this phenomenon masterfully: Swing happens "when all eight oarsmen are rowing in such precise unison that no single action by anyone is out of sync with those of all the others."[13] Every movement matters. Every wrist turn counts. Every back must bend in harmony.

Coach Ulbrickson followed a process similar to our five steps of property optimization:

1. Clarify what you have. He evaluated every rower's capabilities.
2. Connect the pieces. He tested endless combinations in the boat.
3. Collect the data. He ran time trials, observed patterns, and noted the results.
4. Coordinate the elements. He trained the team rigorously.
5. Achieve control. He changed the coxswain.

This process allowed his young team's boat to move powerfully and in harmony, as if by magic.

Ulbrickson never stopped experimenting—mixing and matching rowers, trying different combinations until he found the right chemistry. Some days, he would move one rower out and try another in his spot, always seeking that elusive synchronization. Each change was carefully evaluated, and each result was meticulously considered. Coach, coxswain (the crew member who steers the boat and coordinates the rowers), and crew became

---

13 Daniel James Brown, *The Boys in the Boat: Nine Americans and Their Epic Quest for Gold at the 1936 Berlin Olympics* (Viking Press, 2013).

continued

completely aligned around one goal: making the boat go as fast and efficiently as possible.

When it all finally came together, according to Brown, observers described the Washington crew as "a poem of motion." They had achieved something beyond mere coordination—they had found their swing.

After dominating the prestigious Poughkeepsie Regatta in New York in 1936, they achieved a stunning victory at the Olympic Trials. Their next stop was Nazi Germany for the infamous Berlin Olympics. Hitler expected German dominance in rowing. The Italian team looked unbeatable. The Washington crew? Just working-class boys from Seattle.

But they had their swing. The Olympic final proved it. From behind, they surged past the Italians, past the Germans, until this American crew claimed gold. Their extraordinary coordination had defeated crews with every advantage. Better facilities didn't matter. More funding meant nothing. Precise execution had won the day.

When everything aligns precisely—when every element works in complete coordination and control—seemingly impossible achievements become possible. The lesson for property owners is clear. A property, like a rowing shell, needs harmony. Every system matters. All data flows must align. Controls must be responsive to conditions. When you achieve this state, your property runs on autopilot. You've found the real estate version of swing.

The 1936 Olympic team's success wasn't luck. It wasn't raw talent. It was a process: experimentation and observation, followed by excellence pursued relentlessly.

Now it's your turn to get in the cox's seat. Call your stroke count. Set your rhythm. Help your people, systems, and data find their swing. Then watch your property perform like a gold medal crew—every element moving in synchronized, profitable harmony.

Key Takeaways for Real Estate

Like the 1936 US Olympic rowing team, successful real estate operators need to:

- Perfect execution through extensive experimentation.
- Find the right combination of elements.
- Gain control through complete systems collaboration.
- Strive for self-sustaining, automatic operations.
- Achieve both individual capability and perfect team coordination.

TRANSFORMING DATA INTO STRATEGY AND PERFORMANCE

Just as a championship-level team constantly monitors field conditions and players' actions during a game, property owners need to keep a close watch on their data flows. Systems change. Software undergoes updates. What worked brilliantly yesterday might need attention today. The key is to monitor the playing field and focus on your metrics so you can spot these issues and make adjustments before they impact your property's performance.

Monitoring the Playing Field

If you think of your data flows like players on the field, you'd have the star performers, whose systems are operating smoothly, delivering data exactly as intended; the walking wounded, whose systems are showing signs of stress but still functioning; and the benched players, whose systems have stopped communicating entirely or are outdated.

But when data stops flowing, the causes aren't always obvious. Sometimes, it's simple—like a system running out of storage space. Other times, it's more complex—like a break in the communication chain.

For example, with a property's WiFi system, a single failed access point might go unnoticed by tenants initially, because a well-designed system simply connects users to another nearby access point, unbeknownst to them. But this silent failure reduces the system's capacity and resilience. When that area experiences high demand, or if another nearby access point fails, tenants suddenly face connectivity issues. If concentrated in high-traffic areas, even a small number of failed access points—less than 1 percent of the total system—can dramatically undermine the tenant experience.

This illustrates why proactive digital infrastructure monitoring matters. If you choose not to do it, select a vendor that will. The impact of system failures—any system—isn't just about raw numbers; it's about where and how those failures occur. A property's digital infrastructure requires constant operating vigilance, not just of overall system health but of individual components and **systems interoperability**. Like a coach monitoring player conditioning, property operators need to spot potential weak points before they affect game-day performance.

Effective monitoring requires understanding how your systems communicate. Some systems actively push their data to your central repository, like coaches constantly analyzing and communicating players' positions on the field. Others wait for you to pull data from them, like players waiting for a play call. When a typically chatty system goes quiet, that's an immediate red flag. When a normally responsive system stops answering calls, it's time to investigate.

Your systems need an unbroken connection and clear communication pathways, just like players need clear signals from their coaches. If a wide receiver is unable to hear the quarterback's calls, he may think he's running perfect routes when they're actually the wrong plays. Likewise, a system might generate valuable data, but if the pathway is broken, that information never reaches your command center on game day.

No star athlete or team would wait until game day to check their equipment. By the same logic, property owners shouldn't wait for system failures to check their data flows. Regular digital infrastructure monitoring keeps your systems in championship form, ready to execute when it counts.

Lighting Up the Scoreboard

Just as Coach Ulbrickson's 1936 rowing team found their "swing" through relentless focus and measurement, property owners need precise metrics to achieve peak performance. This isn't the time to chase every opportunity. Like championship teams, you should focus on executing your best plays. And the goal isn't just to collect data, but to aim (like Ulbrickson's crew) for the best possible execution. Keep your eye on the metrics that matter, and let them guide your property to championship performance.

Review metrics that directly tie to your primary goals. Maintaining this focus is crucial, because it's easy to get distracted by low-impact data that seems interesting. Establish clear thresholds that trigger specific actions, and meet regularly with key stakeholders to review progress and adjust strategies. Your metrics should inform your next play, not just tell you the current score. When you focus on forward-looking metrics coupled with current stats, you'll have a much better view of the playing field.

In commercial real estate, three areas typically have the biggest impact on your bottom line: utilities optimization, vacancy management, and insurance cost control. Think of these as three significant phases of your game where you can impact performance. Each requires its own specific metrics and tracking systems.

- **Utilities optimization** often shows early wins, but maintaining and expanding these gains requires comprehensive tracking. Don't just look at total consumption—monitor patterns throughout the day, analyze costs per square foot, and identify peak usage periods. Understanding systems efficiencies and calculating ROI on optimization efforts helps justify further investments in improvement. These metrics tell you not just how much you're spending but where your best opportunities for improvement lie.

- **Vacancy management** isn't just about filling empty spaces—it's about keeping your current tenants happy. Think of tenant retention like maintaining a championship roster: It's always more cost-effective to keep your current players than it is to recruit new ones. Track tenant satisfaction systematically, monitor renewal rates, and measure how quickly you respond to maintenance requests. Understanding space utilization and amenity usage helps you provide what tenants truly value, not just what you think they want.

- **Insurance cost control** often seem like a one-way street, with premiums only going up. But with the right metrics and systems in place, you can change the game. Track your incident response times and detection system performance. Monitor early warning systems for issues like water leaks. Document your prevention program effectiveness and maintain a detailed claims history. These metrics demonstrate to underwriters that you're actively managing risks, not just hoping to avoid them.

Your dashboard should bring all these metrics together in real time where possible, making them accessible to key team members. Think of it as your live game-cast displaying all the stats in real time, with each metric connecting directly to actions you can take. When a metric crosses a predetermined threshold, your team and systems should know exactly what play to call.

Here are some examples.

- **Electric utility bills** (particularly time-of-use or demand charges). Set demand charges thresholds. If an electric bill exceeds your threshold, delegate a team to investigate what drove that surcharge. Was it motor starts? Was it resistance driven? Was something needlessly operating out of time scope? Locate the origin, then focus on avoiding that charge going forward. After each occurrence, build controls into your systems to circumvent such out-of-budget billings moving forward.

- **Vacancy trends.** Of course you already review vacancy stats regularly with your team. In search of trends, also review trailing twelve months' data and other historical tendencies. Seek forward-looking KPIs rather than looking solely at current stats. If vacancy drops below your threshold (or seems likely to drop, based on your trend analysis), inform your marketing and leasing teams and your building engineer. Also, consider the tools and strategies you could use to increase occupancy at a particular site. Through analyzing forward-looking trends and ensuring proactive team involvement, you can avoid or quickly address those dreaded occupancy drops.

- **Insurance premiums.** Be proactive about setting premium budget goals, for both current and future years, and be transparent with the underwriter. Also set premium increase thresholds. Schedule regular reviews with your insurance agents and underwriters. If you get a premium notice above your target, reach out to the underwriter again—before the new rates apply—and request another review. Even if denied, you've made your claim for lower increases next period. Ask the carriers what would reduce such increases going forward; then build reporting and controls into your systems to deliver those and minimize out-of-scope premium increases.

There's both an art and a science to this process. The science lies in the systematic collection and analysis of data; the art is in the interpretation and action. Sometimes the numbers tell you one story, but your experience suggests something different. Trust both. Develop hypotheses based on data, but don't ignore your team's instincts about your properties and the market.

Think of your current metrics like the University of Washington crew's stroke count—they tracked what mattered for achieving perfect synchronization, and nothing more. Focus your attention on the numbers that truly impact your success. Let the rest, however interesting, remain peripheral. In the game of property performance, knowing the right numbers to watch—and act on—makes the difference between average players and champions.

Making Game-Time Adjustments

Once you understand your data flows, tough decisions await. Return to your triangle offense (discussed in chapter 3)—the interplay of process, people, and technology. Your data flows have revealed which systems are contributing to your success and which are holding you back. Now it's time to make strategic adjustments.

Not every system will be playing at a championship level. Some "players" may need coaching up. Others might need to be traded out. And a few should stay on the bench while you focus on your star players. Consider the example of an HVAC system on your property. It might be a strong player, capable of delivering significant energy savings and improved tenant comfort. But if it can't accept external commands—"coaching," so to speak—its potential remains untapped. This is where the art and science of operations management intersect. The science tells you the system's importance. The art lies in deciding whether this uncommunicative system should be upgraded or simply replaced.

This can be a tough choice: Do you move forward with the systems that are already performing well, or do you invest time and resources in bringing a key system up to speed? Think of a property's lighting control system that's currently isolated from your data ecosystem. It's like having a talented player who doesn't know the playbook. The potential impact is there, but reaching it requires investment.

Notably, an early example of visionary thinking about utility optimization can be seen in the Bankside Yards project in London. This property has a network that combines heating and cooling to "balance energy within each building and then between buildings by collecting unwanted heat, say from a refrigerator in a restaurant or a piece of office equipment that needs to be cooled, and carrying that heat to somewhere that needs hot water or domestic heating."[14] While you don't need to be as revolutionary as the Bankside Yards team, you'll need to consider the same factors when making adjustment decisions. Here are a few of them:

- **Current performance impact.** Is the system limiting your property's performance? A system might be functional but holding back your overall optimization efforts. Just as a team might function with an outdated playbook, your property can operate with legacy systems—but at what cost to performance?

- **Potential return on investment.** What improvements could you achieve by upgrading or replacing a system? Is the system a needle mover that can dramatically impact property performance when functioning optimally? The investment might be substantial to get there, but so too should be the returns.

- **Data flow and assimilation capability.** Is this system a team player? Can the system be brought into your coordinated operation? Some systems can be upgraded to accept external commands. Others might require complete replacement. Understanding these technical requirements helps inform your decision-making.

- **Strategic timing.** When is the right time to make changes? Sometimes it makes sense to move forward with what you

---

14 Peter Wilson, "A Next Generation Approach to Heating and Cooling Buildings," *New York Times*, September 25, 2024, https://www.nytimes.com/2024/09/25/climate/fifth-generation-heat-pumps.html.

have while planning future upgrades. Other situations might demand immediate action. Like a coach making substitutions, timing these changes can be crucial to success.

Not every system needs to be a star player immediately. In the early stages of your data-driven transformation, it's often better to focus on getting wins with your already capable systems while developing a longer-term strategy for others. This is where the art of data-driven operations management truly shows—knowing when to push forward with what you have and when to invest in upgrades.

Think of it like building a championship team. You start with your best players and your proven plays. You get some wins on the board. Then you strategically develop or acquire additional talent to strengthen your lineup. Each property will have its own optimal sequence of improvements, driven by its specific conditions and opportunities.

The key is making these decisions systematically rather than reactively. Your Data & Digital Infrastructure Audit should have identified which systems can accept external controls. Use this information, combined with your current performance data, to make strategic decisions about system improvements that work best for your properties. This systematic approach to adjustments helps ensure that each change moves you closer to your goals.

Whether you decide to upgrade an existing system or implement a completely new solution, each move should be part of your larger strategy for optimizing operations. Like a well-coached team, your property should get stronger with each adjustment, building toward championship-level, peak performance.

MAINTAINING PEAK PERFORMANCE

Championship teams don't just win one game—they perform consistently at the highest level throughout the season. The same principle applies to property operations. Maintaining peak performance requires disciplined monitoring, clear communication, timely adjustments, and regular reviews.

Track performance monthly, quarterly, and annually to create a clear picture of trends. Without consistent measurement, you can't know if you're moving toward your goals or drifting off course. These timestamps create your performance history and inform your future strategy. That's because analysis goes beyond collecting numbers—it's about understanding the story they tell. When utility costs spike or tenant satisfaction drops, what's driving those changes? These trends are like game films, revealing patterns that might not be visible in the moment.

Transparency with your team amplifies positive results, so share relevant data with the staff members who can act on it. Maintenance teams often spot patterns in system performance that aren't obvious in the raw numbers. Property managers might identify opportunities that only become clear with access to trend data. Different perspectives lead to better insights.

When metrics trend negatively, quick action is essential. This might mean adjusting system settings, updating procedures, or reconsidering your approach. Sometimes existing systems simply can't deliver the performance you need. Like a team upgrading equipment, properties occasionally need new infrastructure vendors or critical capital improvements.

A systematic approach to maintaining peak performance includes:

- **Regular performance reviews.** Establish a rhythm of performance checks at different intervals. Daily monitoring catches immediate issues. Weekly reviews spot emerging trends. Monthly and quarterly analyses guide strategic decisions.

- **Dashboards and documentation.** Track both numbers and context. What changes have you implemented? What external factors affect performance? This historical record prevents repetition of past mistakes and guides future improvements.

- **Team engagement.** Make performance data accessible and meaningful to those who can use it. Your staff should understand not just what's happening but why it matters. This creates a culture of continuous improvement. .

- **Proactive maintenance.** Don't wait for systems to fail. Regular maintenance and updates keep your systems operating at their best. This includes both digital and physical systems as well as data infrastructure.

- **Response protocols.** When metrics indicate problems, your team should know exactly how to respond. Clear procedures should guide both immediate fixes and longer-term solutions.

Maintaining peak performance is an ongoing process. Regular monitoring leads to better insights, enabling smarter decisions that improve performance. This self-reinforcing cycle of excellence transforms a property from an occasional high performer into a consistent champion.

A PEAK PERFORMANCE PLAYBOOK

Vance and Vicki's journey through the 5C Framework—Clarify, Connect, Collect, Coordinate, and Control—was transforming both their properties and their vision for the future. Like when a championship team is hitting its stride, their experimental plays were turning into consistent wins.

On Vicki's new multifamily development, VRE's greenfield strategy was already paying dividends. By designing digital infrastructure from the ground up, they achieved a $780-per-unit reduction in capital expenses while simultaneously creating massive new revenue streams. Their seamless, secure, private, managed WiFi and technology services weren't just cutting costs—they were enhancing the tenant experience and creating sustainable new income sources to the tune of $690 annual NOI per door.

Meanwhile, Vance's brownfield office property was showing equally impressive results. By taking control of the property's digital infrastructure, VRE managed to capture 43 percent of their tenants for enhanced, high-margin technology services. This meant significant and new recurring revenue of $0.92 annual NOI per square foot. The property wasn't just running more efficiently—it was generating entirely new revenue streams.

"It's like we've found our swing," Vicki said during their weekly strategy session with the OpticWise consultants. "Every system is moving in harmony."

Dave nodded. "That's exactly right. You've gone beyond just collecting data. You're controlling it. Using it. Your properties are responding to your calls like a well-coached team."

"But here's the really exciting part: This is just the beginning," Kaylie added. "With ownership and control of your data and digital infrastructure, you're building something bigger than efficient buildings. You're developing a self-managing portfolio."

Vance leaned forward. "Self-managing?"

"Think about it," Dave explained. "Your systems are communicating. Responding. Learning. You're not just running properties anymore—you're orchestrating an intelligent portfolio that can anticipate needs and respond automatically."

An "intelligent portfolio," he explained, refers to a portfolio where each property operates its own ecosystem within the data-driven confines standardized by your team. Each property has the process, people, and technology to make decisions and become self-managed.

"When taken to the next level," Dave continued, "Victors Real Estate Group can and should own a self-managing portfolio."

"Which means," Vicki exclaimed, "we can focus on higher-level strategy instead of day-to-day operations."

"Exactly," Kaylie confirmed. "You're not just operating better buildings. You're creating a platform for sustained excellence."

As Vance and Vicki left that meeting, they knew they'd crossed an important threshold. They weren't just property owners and managers anymore. They were team builders, creating an organization capable of operating a peak-performing portfolio. Their playbook wasn't just about winning one game—it was about building a dynasty.

The game plan was clear: maintain momentum, keep refining systems, and build a team that could execute at the highest level. They had learned the most important lesson in both sports and business: True champions don't just achieve excellence—they sustain it.

Their journey to peak performance was just beginning. But with clear communication channels among their systems, strong monitoring protocols, and a team aligned around data-driven decision-making, they were ready for the next challenge: turning their initial victories into sustained championship performance.

CHAPTER 5 TAKEAWAYS

1. Master system communication. Understand how to speak the language of your operating systems, and establish clear command channels.

2. Focus on big cost centers. Target your three biggest impact areas—utilities, vacancies, and insurance—with strategic controls.

3. Monitor data flows. Establish systematic tracking of what's flowing, what's bumpy, and what's not working in your systems.

4. Make strategic adjustments. Learn when to upgrade systems, when to replace them, and when to work with what you have using the triangle offense of process, people, and technology.

5. Track key metrics. Implement clear performance measures and thresholds that trigger specific actions.

6. Build team transparency. Share relevant data with staff members who can act on it, and ensure everyone understands their role.

7. Maintain momentum. Create regular review cycles and response protocols to sustain peak performance.

TAKE ACTION

Create your own "playing field" monitoring system by establishing thresholds and response protocols one of your three biggest cost centers—utilities, vacancies, and insurance. Define specific metrics to track and actions to take when thresholds are crossed. This crucial step will help you move from data analysis to active control of your property operations.

Champion: Peak-Performing People and Portfolios

"Isn't life about determining your own finish line?
This journey has always been about reaching your own other shore
no matter what it is, and the dream continues."

—**Diana Nyad,** record-setting Hall of Fame long-distance swimmer

BUILDING PORTFOLIO-WIDE EXCELLENCE

A year after their first meeting with OpticWise, the energy was noticeably different at Victors Real Estate Group. Vance and Vicki had come a long way from their early meetings about data and digital infrastructure. The blueprints and financial reports that had once overwhelmed them had been translated into clear action plans. Strategic sticky notes on the walls of their conference room marked key victories and next steps.

Their two pilot properties had exceeded expectations. The downtown office building showed substantial OpEx reductions, significant new revenues, and a positive annual NOI increase. The new apartment complex is set to come online with impressive CapEx and OpEx reductions due to modern data and digital infrastructure designs and strategies, plus new recurring revenues and a significant NOI increase.

"Remember when we thought we were just in the real estate business?" Vicki mused, reviewing their latest results. "It's amazing what can happen when you get control of your data and digital infrastructure. The numbers don't lie—we're outperforming our projections at both properties."

"But we can't personally drive this transformation across all of our portfolio properties," Vance pointed out, thinking about the long days they'd been working to manage these two test cases. "We'd burn ourselves out trying."

They'd scheduled another meeting with Dave and Kaylie, this time not for technical guidance but for strategic advice. When the OpticWise team arrived, they found Vance and Vicki mapping out their portfolio on a whiteboard, with different properties color-coded by potential and priority.

"We need to scale what we've learned," Vance began, gesturing to their data dashboard. "We're realizing that means we must transform ourselves as leaders, not just change our property operations. The late nights, the constant hands-on management—it's not sustainable at scale."

Dave took in the detailed whiteboard with approval. "Now you're thinking like dynasty builders. Getting these two properties running at peak performance was phase one—proof of concept. Building a peak-performing portfolio is a whole different game. It requires a different level of thinking, a different approach to leadership."

"And it requires a different version of you," Kaylie added, pulling up a chair. "To make this transition successfully, you need to work *on* your business, not *in* it. That means delegating, building the right team, and having the discipline to let go. You'll also need the stamina—both mental and physical—to operate at a higher level."

Vance and Vicki relaxed momentarily in their chairs, relieved to hear Kaylie articulating the fatigue they had been feeling after another long week.

Dave chimed in, "Right now, you're like assistant coaches on the field, deep in the weeds of running the plays. To build and sustain a championship organization, you need to move up to the skybox, where you can see the whole game."

Vance and Vicki had been so focused on transforming their properties that they hadn't fully considered how much they needed to transform themselves. The long hours, constant problem-solving, and endless support and collaboration that had driven their initial success wouldn't scale—they needed a new approach.

"Think about the great sports dynasties," Dave continued. "They didn't just have good players or successful systems. They had leaders who could see the bigger picture—who built sustainable excellence through vision, strategy, and consistent execution. The Chicago Bulls didn't win six championships just because of Michael Jordan's talent—they won because the owner, Jerry Krause, created a system, a culture, a leadership team, and a sustainable way of winning. That's where you need to focus now."

Vicki perked up, energized by the challenge. "So how do we make that transition? How do we go from running properties to building and operating a dynasty? We've mastered the five *C*'s at the property level—Clarify, Connect, Collect, Coordinate, and Control. What's next?"

"That's the right question," Kaylie smiled. "You're ready for the elusive sixth *C*: Champion. Becoming a champion means becoming the type of leader who can build and sustain excellence across an entire portfolio. Are you ready for that challenge?"

Vance and Vicki had come this far by embracing change and pushing beyond their comfort zone. With additional support from Dave and Kaylie, it was time to push forward again—not just for their properties, but for themselves.

Chapter 6 Goals

This chapter explores the elusive sixth *C*—becoming a Champion. We'll guide you through the transition from property-level success to portfolio-wide excellence. You'll learn to elevate your leadership from tactical execution to strategic vision, building the personal and organizational capabilities needed for sustained, scalable performance.

We'll start with developing your talent pipeline and crafting the clear vision required to build champion-level stamina and a culture of excellence. Drawing lessons from sports dynasties and business leaders who've mastered this transition, you'll discover how to move from working *in* your business to working *on* it, creating systems and teams capable of delivering consistent excellence across your entire portfolio.

SHIFTING FROM THE FIELD TO THE SKYBOX

Every Sunday during football season, owner and general manager Jerry Jones watches the Dallas Cowboys from his skybox. It's not just a luxury view; it's a strategic position. From there, he can see the entire operation. He's not running plays—he's running an organization worth billions. Over the decades, whether the team wins or loses, his franchise maintains its dynasty-level value through clear vision, robust systems, and consistent leadership.

Commercial real estate leaders must make a similar transition, from running plays to running the business toward a successful future. While mastering the five *C*'s of the 5C Framework—Clarify, Connect, Collect, Coordinate, and Control—creates peak-performing properties, achieving a peak-performing *portfolio* demands moving to another level and becoming a true champion. You're no longer just operating properties. You're orchestrating systems. You're building culture. You're developing talent. This elevation in thinking changes everything.

Transforming Your Business

This transformation requires leaders who can build self-managing companies capable of scaling excellence. The journey begins with achieving a "state of flow"—that sweet spot "where people are so involved in an activity that nothing else seems to matter; the experience is so enjoyable that people will continue to do it even at great cost, for the sheer sake of doing it."[15] Just as elite athletes find their zone where performance becomes natural, real estate organizations can achieve this state where excellence becomes automatic. As you evolve into a next-level portfolio leader, your role shifts from direct execution to strategic oversight. When this is done right, more of your work happens in this flow state, and the lines between work, fun, and play begin to blur.

---

15 Mihaly Csikszentmihalyi, *Creativity: Flow and the Psychology of Discovery and Invention* (HarperCollins, 2013).

Champion leadership for a
self-managing portfolio capable
of scaling excellence

Build your talent pipeline

Craft and communicate your vision

Develop champion-level stamina

Create a culture of excellence

Transforming yourself and your business at this level requires you to pay attention to four critical areas—not just one at a time, but in parallel. Think of them as essential to your purpose and function, like the four legs of a stool or four wheels on a car.

The first is *building your talent pipeline*. Champions don't just fill positions—they build a deep and flexible bench of talent ready to perform at a higher level as the organization grows. This means constantly recruiting and identifying people who can grow with your vision. Having the right people ready at the right time becomes crucial for scaling success.

Consider starting with small collaborations before making long-term commitments. Think of it as scouting potential team members through consulting roles or project work. This approach lets both parties test the fit while you build a talent pool ready to scale when opportunities arise.

The second area of transforming business is *crafting and communicating your vision.* Working on the business requires dedicated time for strategic thinking, industry engagement, and stakeholder relationships. As a leader, you are the "chief repetition officer," whose role is to consistently communicate your vision and the company's core values until it all becomes part of your organization's DNA. The language you use shapes how your team thinks and acts.

The Navy SEALs follow a training mantra that works for many different types of complex operations with a lot at stake: *Slow is smooth, smooth is fast.* Take your time as you develop your unique observations and understanding of your organization into a crystal-clear mission and strategy. Partner with trusted advisors who can pressure-test your ideas and help refine your vision. Multiple perspectives can strengthen your foundation and help your best ideas take flight.

The third crucial element here is *developing champion-level stamina.* Leading a championship portfolio demands sustained energy and sharp decision-making. In this context, stamina isn't about working longer hours—it's about building the organization's capacity to make good decisions consistently, day after day, year after year. Like any business skill, this capacity can be systematically developed.

Stamina also applies to you, personally and physically. Prioritize sleep, exercise, and nutrition for yourself. While many other books cover physical wellness in detail, we emphasize and embody this point: Your organization can't perform at its peak if you're not at yours. Your personal energy and wellness management directly impact your business outcomes.

Finally, transform your business by *creating a culture of excellence.* Champion organizations don't just employ good people—they systematically develop them. Build clear growth paths, provide continuous learning opportunities, and foster a culture where improvement becomes automatic. When the culture supports the desired outcomes, excellence becomes your organization's default state.

Invest in hands-on learning experiences. Have your team work alongside mentors who can teach, train, and problem-solve with them. Listen to your employees' aspirations and help them grow in ways that align with your organizational goals.

Transforming Yourself

The skybox perspective requires personal transformation, too. As discussed earlier, you need stamina for long-term success, mental clarity for strategic decisions, and physical wellness for sustained performance. These aren't luxury items. They're essential tools for portfolio-level leadership.

Get in physical shape, and maintain focus on your body's condition and your mental health. If you are physically and mentally strong, so will be your strategy and execution in the business world. And you will be able to recruit even stronger team players.

To further your personal and professional growth, start by engaging a coach. Every uber-successful leader we know has at least one coach, so don't be afraid or ashamed to hire one. After all, nobody can do this alone. Even Michael Jordan had personal coaches and trainers. Find someone who fits your personal and professional standards and will go the distance with you, all in the name of your success.

The shift from property success to portfolio excellence demands more than just doing different things—it requires becoming a different kind of leader. This evolution—from tactical to strategic, from doing to leading, from reacting to anticipating—is essential for building a peak-performing portfolio and is summarized in Figure 7. Transformation doesn't happen overnight, but it does form the foundation of lasting success.

Figure 7. Shifting from the Field to the Skybox

On the Field . . .	In the Skybox . . .
• Tactical execution	• Strategic vision
• Doing the work	• Leading the organization
• Reacting to problems	• Anticipating opportunities
• Working harder	• Working smarter
• Property-level focus	• Portfolio-level perspective
• Individual effort	• Team orchestration
• Managing daily operations	• Building systems and culture

For those willing to make this transition, the rewards extend beyond financial returns. Working *on* the business rather than *in* it creates space for strategic thinking, engaging with stakeholders, and identifying new opportunities. It allows leaders to operate at their highest level while building an organization capable of sustained excellence across the entire portfolio. The work becomes not just manageable but energizing—not just profitable but purposeful.

Your role as a business leader demands disciplined time management. You must create space for strategic thinking. You need time to spot market trends, identify opportunities, and engage with stakeholders. Plus, you're always recruiting—not necessarily hiring, but building your bench. Every conversation becomes a chance to identify future talent.

Managing your personal energy becomes crucial at this level. A strong, research-based framework for this comes from the work of Yale School of Management psychologist Emma Seppälä, who wisely suggests that you stop trying to manage your time and instead focus on managing your energy. She reminds leaders that while "constantly focusing on the next thing or the next person may seem productive, slowing down and being present has far more profound benefits. By being present, you will enter a state of flow that is highly productive."[16] So, learning to balance time for things like rest, exercise, research, reflection, and rocking at work are critical for you to be right here, right now—whatever the moment demands of you.

EVERYONE IS *NOT* DOING IT

Just as the Williams sisters revolutionized tennis through their values-based approach to excellence, today's commercial real estate leaders must realize that a core value of their work is focus on **performance-enhancing data and systems (PEDS)**. That's right, we're deliberately reclaiming this negative acronym from its controversial role in sports history to represent the positive value of something powerful and legitimate—the systematic use of data and integrated systems to achieve unprecedented levels of property performance.

For the past half-century, performance-enhancing drugs (PEDs) have cast a shadow over professional sports. From Major League Baseball's "steroid era" of the 1990s to cycling's doping scandals in the 2000s to ongoing controversies in bodybuilding and fitness,

---

16   Kira M. Newman, "Manage Your Energy, Not Your Time," *Greater Good Magazine*, March 1, 2016, https://greatergood.berkeley.edu/article/item/manage_your_energy_ not_your_time; Emma Seppälä, "How Being Present Increases Your Charisma," *Greater Good Magazine*, February 18, 2016, https://greatergood.berkeley.edu/article/item/ being_present_increases_your_charisma.

GOOD SPORTS: Balance and Brilliance[17]

When Venus and Serena Williams first emerged from the tennis courts of Compton, California, few would have predicted they would revolutionize not just tennis but the very definition of athletic excellence and business success. As Black women in a predominantly White sport, they faced significant resistance. Early headlines labeled Venus a "party crasher." But the sisters remained unapologetically themselves, transforming both their sport and its culture.

The foundation of the sisters' athletic success was physical dominance. They ushered in a new era in women's tennis, bringing power to the game with explosive serves and commanding groundstrokes. Venus reached the US Open finals as an unseeded seventeen-year-old in 1997. Serena would go on to win twenty-three Grand Slam singles titles, while Venus won seven. Together, they claimed fourteen Grand Slam doubles championship titles. Their willingness to challenge conventions while maintaining excellence provides a model for market leadership.

The Williams sisters understood that excellence isn't confined to the court. While maintaining peak athletic performance, they systematically expanded into new arenas. As Venus later reflected, "Balance isn't a destination; it's a way of living. In our hustle-driven world, true success comes from making space for what fuels you and prioritizing your well-being." This philosophy

---

17 Ken Makin, "Serena Williams' Legacy—On and Off the Court," *Christian Science Monitor*, August 29, 2022, https://www.csmonitor.com/Commentary/2022/0829/Serena-Williams-legacy-on-and-off-the-court; Kurt Streeter, "From Start to Finish, Venus and Serena Williams Always Had Each Other," *The New York Times*, September 1, 2022, https://www.nytimes.com/2022/09/01/sports/tennis/serena-venus-williams-doubles.html#:-:text=That%20they%20had%20one%20another,won%20five%20of%20those%20matches; Venus Williams (@venuswilliams), Instagram post, October 8, 2024, https://www.instagram.com/venuswilliams/reel/DA3TqoBxC-P/.

continued

shaped their approach to dynasty building. Venus pioneered equal pay for women tennis players and launched successful fashion and interior design ventures. Serena built a venture capital empire, with investments in eighty-five companies, fourteen of which achieved "unicorn" status: when a private company is valued at over $1 billion.

The Williams' success stemmed from deep wisdom about excellence. Venus has pointed out that "taking a step back isn't a weakness—it's a strategy for long-term success," and the sister took those words to heart. Recognizing that sustainable performance requires careful energy management, they pursued interests outside tennis, which many people initially criticized. This diversification actually extended their careers and developed their business acumen. Like portfolio optimization, they understood that concentration creates vulnerability while diversification builds resilience.

Most important, they leveraged their success to create broader change. Serena's venture fund focuses on underrepresented business founders, with 79 percent of investments going to diverse leaders. Venus's advocacy helped establish equal prize money for women at major tournaments. They understood that true dynasty-building extends beyond personal success. They took their values—specifically, their commitment to equity—into multiple domains to make an impact on whole systems.

The Williams sisters didn't just dominate their sport—they transcended it. Through physical excellence, strategic diversification, and unwavering commitment to impact, they built a multidimensional dynasty that continues to grow. Their example shows that true champions don't just perform at their peak—they expand the way of thinking about peak performance to achieve true excellence across domains.

> ## Key Takeaways for Real Estate
>
> Like the Williams sisters, successful real estate operators need to:
> - Use physical and mental excellence as a foundation for broader success.
> - Balance intense focus and core values with strategic diversification.
> - Challenge industry conventions while maintaining operational excellence.
> - Build systems that create lasting impact beyond individual properties.
> - Leverage success in one domain to create opportunities in others.

PEDs represented a shortcut to success. The excuse is always the same: "Everyone is doing it." But these chemical shortcuts ultimately undermined the integrity of competition and tarnished countless achievements.

Unlike in the sports world, however, by now we realize that most commercial real estate organizations are *not* doing it. In fact, very few modern CRE operators are fully embracing our version of PEDS. Making this a core value for your company makes you an early adopter, which creates a remarkable competitive advantage.

We regularly hear property owners acknowledge the potential of owning their data and digital infrastructure. They say things like, "Even if the numbers were only fifty percent as good as what you're claiming, it would be incredible." Yet many, overwhelmed by daily operations and the perceived complexity of new systems, hesitate to take action.

From the skybox, you will see opportunities that others miss. Deal pipeline development will become a core focus. You'll be able to spot emerging markets, identify undervalued assets, and recognize trends before they become obvious. This higher-level view transforms how you approach growth and sets you apart from the pack.

Unlike their controversial namesake, these PEDS offer legitimate enhancement that benefits owners, tenants, and the industry as a whole. For those who commit to making this shift in commercial real estate, the competitive advantage is clear—and growing. Early adopters are building capabilities that traditional approaches cannot match. The question isn't *whether* to embrace PEDS—it's *how quickly* you can develop these capabilities before they become industry standard.

When Jerry Jones invested more than $1 billion (over twice the original budget) in the new AT&T Stadium with that massive scoreboard, critics called him crazy. Now, it's the industry standard. No matter how the Cowboys perform on the field, the franchise is worth seventy-three times what Jones paid for it in 1989.[18] That's skybox thinking: seeing beyond current norms, building for the future while others focus on the present, and making bold moves based on clear vision.

The transition to this type of thinking isn't easy. Many leaders struggle to delegate. They miss the hands-on work. They are not disciplined about focusing and amplifying their core message. But this elevation is essential: If you're intending to build a dynasty, your organization needs you in the skybox, not on the field.

---

18 Michael Ozanian, "The Cowboys Are Worth $11 Billion: Here's How Dallas Went from Losing $1 Million a Month to Topping the NFL in Value," *CNBC Sport*, September 5, 2024, https://www.cnbc.com/2024/09/05/dallas-cowboys-most-valuable-nfl-team.html.

CONSTANT EVOLUTION IS THE GOAL

Success breeds opportunity. The insights gained from optimizing one property type often illuminate possibilities in others. And smart leaders are always looking ahead. They see beyond their current portfolio. They explore new verticals. They push boundaries personally and professionally.

Affordable housing is one example. Many dismiss this market as unprofitable. Yet we recently met with a property group that was building several 400-to-500-unit developments across three states. They typically hold these properties for ten years and are making significant returns. The group's success comes from applying sophisticated data and systems approaches to a traditionally overlooked market.

Senior living presents similar opportunities, and student housing offers unique challenges and rewards. Each vertical demands its own optimization strategy, but the fundamental principles remain constant: Data drives decisions. Systems enable efficiency. Clear thinking reveals opportunities that others miss. Success comes to those who are willing to evolve.

Market adaptation requires focused and adaptable leaders. You must uphold core principles while exploring new approaches. Your organization needs to be both stable and flexible. This balance comes from having strong systems and capable teams. Your processes should be robust enough to maintain excellence while incorporating new insights. Strategic refinement isn't a sprint—it's a marathon.

To stay in the game for the long haul, you'll need sustained clarity for evaluating opportunities and mental sharpness for decision-making. You'll also need a systematic approach to analyzing performance across your entire portfolio. The same AI and data-driven methods that transformed individual properties can revolutionize how you evaluate and optimize your portfolio's financial performance.

The most successful organizations maintain a continuous improvement mindset, applying analytics at both the property and portfolio levels. Championship-level CRE owners aggregate financial data across properties, looking for patterns and opportunities that might be invisible when viewing assets in isolation. Never satisfied with their current performance, they're always seeking insights by combining previously siloed data—from operational metrics to market conditions to financial returns.

Small optimizations compound over time, whether in building operations or portfolio composition. Minor adjustments in asset allocation or property positioning, informed by comprehensive data analysis, can lead to major advantages in overall portfolio performance. And the results speak for themselves: Organizations led from the skybox develop more vital systems. They build deeper benches. They move more quickly on opportunities. They maintain consistent performance across entire portfolios. Most important, they build sustainable excellence that outlasts any individual property's success.

Your strategy should evolve like a living document. Review it regularly. Test assumptions and question conventions. The market doesn't stand still; neither should your approach. To achieve portfolio-wide excellence, you must continually evolve as a leader and invest in yourself on the physical, mental, and emotional levels. But evolution doesn't mean instability. It means thoughtful adaptation based on clear evidence and careful analysis.

The goal isn't just to grow bigger—it's to grow better, smarter, more efficient. This requires discipline, focus, and clear thinking. The organizations that thrive don't just *chase* opportunities—they *generate* them through consistent excellence and strategic innovation.

Your skybox awaits. The view will transform how you see and operate your business. But remember: The goal isn't to escape the work. It's to elevate your impact . . . to build something bigger than yourself . . . to create a legacy of excellence that defines true dynasty-level success.

HAIL TO THE VICTORS!

Building a true dynasty in commercial real estate isn't just about property performance. It's about personal excellence, organizational greatness, and leadership commitment. Like any champion, you must dedicate yourself to peak performance in every domain.

The CRE organizations that succeed share a collection of common traits: They commit to total transformation. They improve their physical wellness to handle long days. They sharpen their mental clarity to make better decisions. They build strong teams through consistent leadership. They develop robust systems through careful attention. They trust data-driven decisions over habitual, unsubstantiated practices.

Vance and Vicki embodied this commitment to transformation. Six months after their initial realization about scaling their success, they had made significant changes. They were no longer working twelve-hour days, trying to manage everything themselves. Instead, they had built a strong team and implemented robust systems that allowed them to focus on strategic growth.

Working with Dave and Kaylie of OpticWise, they developed a systematic approach to portfolio transformation. They started with themselves, developing the stamina needed for sustained leadership. Working with a coach, they implemented personal workout routines and set aside time for professional development and strategic thinking. They learned to trust their team, delegate effectively, and maintain the big-picture perspective needed for portfolio-level success.

"The biggest change," Vicki reflected during a strategy session, "isn't in our properties—it's in us. We're not just managing buildings anymore. We're building a dynasty."

Vance nodded in agreement. "Remember how overwhelmed we felt while trying to handle everything ourselves? Now, we have systems in place, a strong team, and a clear vision. We're actually enjoying the journey."

The keys to sustainable success that Vance and Vicki discovered were straightforward:

- Maintain physical wellness for consistent energy.
- Develop mental clarity for strategic thinking.
- Build strong teams through careful, constant selection.
- Create robust systems for reliable performance.
- Trust data-driven decisions for optimal results.

Each element reinforces the others: Physical wellness supports mental clarity. Mental clarity enables better decisions and superior team development. Strong teams implement robust systems. Robust systems generate reliable data. Reliable data drives better decisions. And the cycle continues, building momentum with each iteration.

The opportunity before you is extraordinary. The tools for transformation are available. The path to excellence is clear. The question is: Are you ready to become the leader your dynasty needs? Are you prepared to transform yourself as thoroughly as your properties? Are you committed to the journey of total excellence?

Your dynasty awaits—rooted not just in property performance or portfolio value, but in the lasting impact of leadership excellence. Begin with yourself. Extend to your team. Expand across your portfolio. This is how real estate dynasties are built: one leader, one property, one improvement at a time.

As Vance and Vicki discovered, the journey to peak performance starts now. Are you ready to build a peak-performing property portfolio that stands the test of time?

CHAPTER 6 TAKEAWAYS

1. Elevate your perspective. Transform your leadership approach from tactical to strategic, by moving from the field to the sky-box position for portfolio-wide vision.

2. Build your bench. Develop robust talent pipelines and succession plans that enable sustainable growth and systematic excellence across your organization.

3. Optimize your energy. Cultivate the physical stamina, mental clarity, and personal wellness practices needed for sustained, portfolio-level leadership.

4. Craft and convey a clear vision. Create and consistently communicate a compelling direction that becomes deeply embedded in your organization's DNA.

5. Enhance performance systematically. Implement performance-enhancing data and systems as a legitimate competitive advantage in your market.

6. Foster excellence. Create a culture of continuous improvement through systematic development of people, processes, and capabilities.

7. Balance focus and flexibility. Maintain intense concentration on core operations while pursuing strategic diversification to build resilient organizations.

8. Drive continuous improvement. Establish stable, scalable systems while maintaining a mindset of constant refinement and evolution.

9. Prioritize personal development. Recognize that your own wellness, energy management, and leadership growth are essential business investments.

TAKE ACTION

Regularly secure dedicated weekly blocks on your calendar for personal wellness activities, strategic thinking and planning, and private time. Document these commitments in your calendar and protect them as rigorously as you would any other business priority.

The 5C Framework for Peak Property Performance

S ports dynasties aren't built overnight. The same is true of commercial real estate success. Transforming your properties into high-performing assets is a journey. Each of the five *C*'s (listed as follows) builds upon the previous ones, creating a foundation for long-term success. Start with *Clarity*, build *Connections*, *Collect* your data, *Coordinate* your team, and take *Control* of your future.

Once you work through this framework, there is a sixth *C* that is the outcome of your hard work. You and your team become... *Champions*.

CLARIFY (Entering the Arena)

See your properties through a new lens. Just as championship teams start with thorough scouting reports, you'll begin by conducting a complete Data & Digital Infrastructure Audit (DDIA). This comprehensive assessment covers everything from network infrastructure to tenant experience systems, giving you complete clarity on your digital assets and untapped opportunities.

Key Actions

- Catalog all systems and data sources.
- Identify inefficiencies and redundancies.
- Evaluate current digital infrastructures.
- Assess data ownership status.

 ## CONNECT (Developing Your Playbook)

Break down the silos. Like a championship team that needs every player working together, your property systems should operate as one cohesive unit. Utilize the Data and Digital Infrastructure Prioritization Chart to assess your current systems. Transform isolated systems into a consolidated digital nervous system that maximizes efficiency and performance.

Key Actions

- Connect to standalone systems.
- Consolidate redundant networks.
- Create secure data pathways.
- Establish system communication protocols.

COLLECT (Building the Best Team)

Assemble your championship roster. Build a team and culture that understands the power of data. Create a centralized data lake that you own and control, bringing together information from every aspect of your operations. Leverage the triangle offense for CRE: process, people, and technology.

Key Actions

- Foster a data-driven culture.
- Train staff on new systems.
- Implement data governance.
- Establish data ownership.

COORDINATE (Preseason Training)

Transform individual talents into a winning team. Like a well-oiled sports franchise, all of your systems and people need to work from the same playbook. Connect and control with AI, creating an intelligent environment where your building can anticipate and respond to needs in real time.

Key Actions

- Synchronize operations.
- Automate routine tasks.
- Implement predictive maintenance.
- Enable real-time adjustments.

CONTROL (It's Game Time)

Take command of your operations. With everything connected and coordinated, start making data-driven decisions that impact your bottom line. Control through communication, focusing first on the most impactful plays. Use real-time dashboards to monitor performance and spot opportunities across your portfolio.

Key Actions

- Monitor key metrics.
- Make data-driven decisions.
- Optimize operations.
- Drive strategic initiatives.

 ## CHAMPION (Peak-Performing People and Portfolios)

Elevate your leadership from property operator to portfolio visionary. Like a coach moving from the field to the skybox, you'll shift from tactical execution to strategic oversight. Build an organization capable of sustaining excellence across your entire portfolio, through robust systems and a culture of continuous improvement.

Key Actions

- Build your talent pipeline.
- Craft and communicate a clear vision.
- Develop champion-level stamina.
- Create a culture of excellence.

The true mark of a champion isn't just having high-performing properties—it's building a sustainable dynasty that continues to innovate and excel in an ever-evolving market. Through the systematic use of performance-enhancing data and systems, you'll maintain a legitimate competitive advantage that transforms not just your properties, but your entire organization.

As the famous proverb suggests, a journey of a thousand miles begins with one step. Begin your journey with the DDIA in appendix B to see where you stand today (or call OpticWise to help you with the process). This is the first step toward charting your path to championship performance.

Data & Digital Infrastructure Audit (DDIA)

To truly see your properties in new ways, use our Data & Digital Infrastructure Audit (DDIA) tool. This comprehensive inventory covers everything from network infrastructure to data analytics.

Data and Digital Infrastructure Domain (Including Various Elements)	What do you want to accomplish with the tool?	Does it meet your requirements?	Is the contract aligned?	Who owns the data? How is it accessed?	Is it private with strong security?
Network infrastructure and internet of things (IoT) • Asset tracking systems • Common area WiFi • Internet circuit(s) • Noise level sensors • Occupancy sensors • Smart technology • Temperature and humidity sensors • Tenant spaces WiFi • Voice services					

Data and Digital Infrastructure Domain (Including Various Elements)	What do you want to accomplish with the tool?	Does it meet your requirements?	Is the contract aligned?	Who owns the data? How is it accessed?	Is it private with strong security?
Security, Access Control, and Risk Management • Access controls • Environmental compliance monitoring • Insurance management • Intrusion detection • Keys management • Regulatory compliance tracking • Safety and emergency systems • Smart locks • Surveillance • Video recording					
Energy, Environmental Management, and Sustainability • Air handlers • Air quality monitors • BMS/BAS (environmental) • Carbon footprint tracking • Capital equipment usage • Energy management • EV charging • Green building certification management • HVAC optimization • Indoor air quality management • Leak detection • Potable water systems • Power quality • Smart lighting • Smart thermostats • Solar systems • Submetering: electric • Submetering: gas • Utility metering • Utility water • Waste management systems • Water management • Wellness certification systems					

Data and Digital Infrastructure Domain (Including Various Elements)	What do you want to accomplish with the tool?	Does it meet your requirements?	Is the contract aligned?	Who owns the data? How is it accessed?	Is it private with strong security?
Property Operations and Tenant Experience • Amenity booking systems • Campuswide WiFi experience • Community engagement tools • Concierge services • Facilities management • Feedback and survey systems • Occupancy analytics • Parking management • Property management • Room scheduling • Tenant communication platforms • Tenant management • Vendor management					
Financial and Asset Management • Asset valuation tools • Expense tracking • Investment performance analytics • Predictive maintenance scheduling • Rent collection systems					
Data Aggregation and Analytics • Benchmarking tools • Business intelligence platforms • Capital equipment usage • Custom reporting systems • Market trend analysis • Other smart technologies • Predictive analytics					

AI 101: Understanding the Basics

To effectively engage with artificial intelligence (AI) technologies in commercial real estate, and to support positive engagements with stakeholders, a basic understanding of key concepts and components of AI—and its relation to business intelligence (BI)—is essential.

THE THREE PILLARS OF AI

AI consists of three essential components that work together to create intelligent systems.

Natural language processing (NLP) enables computers to understand, process, and respond to human language. Think of it as the technology that allows AI to read tenant communications, analyze maintenance requests, or read and input vendor invoices. NLP can perform various other CRE tasks, from analyzing sentiment in tenant feedback to summarizing lengthy documents to translating communications into different languages.

Machine learning (ML) is what allows AI systems to improve their performance and learn from their experiences. Unlike traditional programming where every rule must be explicitly defined, ML systems can learn from data to identify patterns and make predictions. What makes ML particularly powerful is its ability to process massive amounts of data and discover insights that might not be apparent to human analysts. In CRE operations, ML can analyze historical data to predict maintenance needs, optimize energy usage, and forecast market trends.

Robotic process automation (RPA) represents the "doing" (not just "thinking") part of AI—it's the technology that automates manual and repetitive tasks. Robots can perform routine virtual operations like data entry, report generation, or system updates, as well as emulate human actions, all at a high level of accuracy and speed. In CRE operations, RPA can handle everything from processing lease applications to scheduling and performing maintenance tasks to updating tenant records.

AI AND BUSINESS INTELLIGENCE: A POWERFUL PARTNERSHIP

AI and BI are distinct yet complementary technologies that should work together to greatly enhance decision-making capabilities. BI focuses on collecting, organizing, and visualizing data to understand performance, while AI takes this further by proactively identifying patterns to predict future outcomes and suggest actions. Together, they provide a complete toolkit for operations management and optimization.

BI comprises a human component, which includes the people within an organization who are responsible for creating, accessing, interpreting, and utilizing data systems and outputs. AI is an augmentation to BI and can automate repetitive tasks in the BI process, such as data cleaning and feature engineering, freeing up human analysts to focus on higher-level decision-making. And AI algorithms can uncover complex relationships within data that might be missed by humans and by traditional BI methods, leading to deeper and more valuable insights.

Consider this analogy: BI is like a detailed map of where your property portfolio has been. AI is like a GPS that can not only indicate where you've been but also suggest the best routes forward and warn you about potential obstacles ahead.

This combination of BI and AI enables CRE owners, operators, and managers to:

- Analyze historical performance data.
- Predict future trends and needs.
- Automate routine tasks.
- Generate deeper insights from available data.
- Make more informed strategic decisions.

Understanding these fundamentals helps owners, operators, and managers better evaluate and implement AI solutions in their operations, ensuring they can effectively leverage these powerful tools for sustainable competitive advantages.

Data Lakes versus Data Warehouses

C hapter 3 introduced the fundamental differences between data lakes and data warehouses.

Data warehouses are like organized filing cabinets—they store structured data in predetermined formats. Think of your access control logs or tenant payment records, where every piece of information fits into clearly defined categories. They're excellent for routine business reporting but limited in their flexibility.

Data lakes, by contrast, are more like digital reservoirs that can hold any type of information. They can store structured data (like those access logs), semi-structured data (like maintenance reports with varying free-form entries), and unstructured data (like email content) all in one place. They offer more flexibility but require more sophisticated management.

Consider a data warehouse as a baseball scorecard with specific statistics to record, and a data lake as a blank notepad where observers record anything interesting they notice during the game. The scorecard provides consistent, easily analyzable data, while the notepad might capture unexpected insights but requires more effort to analyze.

Figure 8 provides a quick guide to help you understand the differences between the two ways of storing data, followed by the essential steps of building your own data lake. Whether you choose to build in-house, adopt a hybrid approach, or partner with a vendor, you'll find practical guidance for each stage of the journey.

UNDERSTANDING THE BASICS

A data warehouse is like a highly organized library with a strict cataloging system. It stores structured, processed data in a predefined format. A data lake is a vast reservoir that can hold any type of data in its original form. It can store structured data, semi-structured data, and unstructured data all in one place.

Figure 8. Data Lakes vs. Data Warehouses: Strengths and Weaknesses

Feature	Data Warehouse	Data Lake
Data Structure	Organized, structured data	Any type of data: structured, semi-structured, or unstructured
Flexibility	Limited: follows preset schemas	Highly flexible: adapts to any data type
Processing Time	Fast for predefined queries	Can be slower for complex analyses
Cost Efficiency	Higher storage costs	Lower storage costs
Scalability	More difficult to scale	Easily scalable
Best Use Cases	Regular reporting, standard analytics	Advanced analytics, AI/ML applications
User Profile	Business analysts, executives	Data scientists, technical analysts
Data Quality	Highly curated, verified	Raw; requires validation during analysis

OPTIONS FOR BUILDING YOUR DATA LAKE

You have three options when creating a data lake: build (in-house), partner (outsource), or buy (hybrid).

Building your own data lake in-house offers ultimate control over your data infrastructure. Advantages include:

- Full customization capability

- No vendor lock-in

- Complete data sovereignty

Disadvantages include:

- Significant technical expertise required

- Higher upfront costs

- Ongoing maintenance responsibility

Partnering with an external vendor to fully outsource your data lake leaves management of your data in the service provider's hands. Advantages include:

- Minimal internal technical requirements

- Rapid deployment

- Predictable costs

Disadvantages include:

- Less control over infrastructure

- Vendor dependency

- Potentially higher long-term costs

Buying a data lake is a hybrid approach that combines in-house control with vendor solutions. Advantages include:

- Balance of control and convenience
- Ability to leverage existing tools while maintaining key operations
- Scalable investment model

Disadvantages include:

- Complex vendor management
- Integration challenges
- Potential compatibility issues

Essential Steps for Establishing Your Data Lake

Whether you're building in-house, deploying a hybrid solution, or partnering with a vendor, here are six essential steps to construct your data lake:

1. Complete a full data inventory and security assessment. Take stock of every data source in your portfolio—from property management systems to IoT sensors to tenant communication platforms. Define precise governance requirements that specify who can access what information and how sensitive data will be protected. Establish robust security protocols that safeguard your information while ensuring compliance with privacy regulations. For a commercial real estate operation, this means mapping everything from access control logs to energy management systems to tenant payment records.

2. Design your data architecture. Map out exactly how data will flow through your organization. Choose your storage solutions and define your data ingestion processes. Think of this like designing your building's utility systems—you need clean, efficient pathways for data to flow from all sources into your central repository. Plan your touch points carefully, considering how different systems—from your HVAC controls to your tenant portals—will connect and share information. Your architecture determines how effectively your data lake will serve your organization's needs.

3. Build your core infrastructure. Construct the foundation of your data lake by setting up the actual systems and tools you've selected. Establish automated data pipelines to move information from various sources into your lake. Configure security and monitoring systems to track performance and identify potential issues. This phase requires careful coordination, similar to managing a major building renovation—everything needs to come together in the right sequence.

4. Implement quality control systems. Implement systems to ensure data accuracy and reliability. Set up validation processes that verify incoming data, whether it's occupancy sensors, energy usage metrics, or maintenance records. Create automated testing protocols to catch issues before they become problems, and develop error-handling processes to manage any issues that do arise. Think of this as your building's preventive maintenance program; it must identify and address problems before they affect operations.

5. Create comprehensive documentation. Develop clear documentation for every aspect of your data lake and data ingress/egress methods. Create user guides that help your team navigate systems effectively. Document technical specifications that detail how everything is connected and configured. Establish clear maintenance procedures that ensure ongoing smooth operation. Just as you maintain detailed plans and operations manuals for your properties, your data lake needs thorough documentation to ensure long-term success.

6. Optimize performance. Monitor and improve your data lake's efficiency. Track performance metrics and adjust resources as needed, much like fine-tuning a building's systems for optimal energy usage. Refine your processes based on actual usage patterns and emerging needs. Pay particular attention to areas where data flow might be bottlenecked or where users have difficulty accessing the information they need.

Keep in mind that building a data lake isn't a one-time project. Think of it more as a continuous operational process that evolves over time alongside your business. As your property portfolio grows and technology advances, your data lake should adapt and grow with you. The goal is to create a flexible, scalable system that can continue to provide valuable insights as your business evolves.

Data and Digital Infrastructure Prioritization Chart

The Data & Digital Infrastructure Audit (DDIA), detailed in appendix B, identifies six key domains, containing a total of sixty-seven elements (more elements exist or will emerge in the future):

- Network infrastructure and IoT: nine elements
- Security, access control, and risk management: ten elements
- Energy, environmental management, and sustainability: twenty-three elements
- Property operations and tenant experience: thirteen elements
- Financial and asset management: five elements
- Data aggregation and analytics: seven elements

Most properties will only have a subset of these elements in place. The goal is first to audit what you have, then to use this Data and

Digital Infrastructure Prioritization Chart to guide discussions and decision-making about where to focus your improvement efforts.

This is a tool for asking structured questions about your infrastructure, not for making absolute judgments. You can easily prioritize what deserves focus using our scoring system. Each element is rated on a scale of 1–5 for each factor, with higher scores indicating higher priority:

Return on investment

- 1 = Low potential for cost savings or revenue generation.
- 5 = High potential for significant financial impact.

Performance issues

- 1 = System works well with minimal issues.
- 5 = System frequently causes problems or inefficiencies.

Data ownership

- 1 = You have full ownership of and access to data.
- 5 = Data is entirely vendor-controlled, with limited access.

Infrastructure ownership

- 1 = You own and control the infrastructure.
- 5 = Infrastructure is entirely vendor-owned and -managed.

Time sensitivity

- 1 = No urgent need for changes.
- 5 = Immediate action is required (e.g., contract expiring, compliance issues).

Here is an example of scoring for one element ("smart technology") from the network infrastructure and IoT domain. A total score of 20/25 would indicate the element deserves significant attention (in this case, the example element is smart technology). The first DDI domain is illustrated below. Apply this method to score each of the six DDI domains and all applicable elements with each domain.

DDI Domain & Element	ROI	Performance Issues	Data Ownership	Infrastructure Ownership	Time Sensitivity	Total Score
Network Infrastructure and IoT	☑	☑	☑	☑	☑	Sum = 20/25
	☐ 1	☐ 1	☐ 1	☐ 1	☐ 1	
☐ Asset tracking systems	☐ 2	☐ 2	☐ 2	☐ 2	☐ 2	
☐ Common area WiFi	☐ 3	☑ 3	☐ 3	☑ 3	☐ 3	
	☐ 4	☐ 4	☐ 4	☐ 4	☑ 4	
☐ Internet circuit(s)	☑ 5	☐ 5	☑ 5	☐ 5	☐ 5	
☐ Noise level sensors						
☐ Occupancy sensors						
☑ Smart technology						
☐ Temperature and humidity sensors						
☐ Tenant spaces WiFi						
☐ Voice services						

We recommend creating a spreadsheet to analyze relevant elements at your property. This systematic approach helps identify priorities objectively across both existing properties (brownfield) and new developments (greenfield).

Don't Play through the Pain: The Case for Doing the Right Thing

This true story begins during the construction of a 350,000-square-foot apartment complex by a property management company. When contractors encountered cable length limitations while installing access control and security systems, they faced a choice: conduct a proper redesign or find a quick fix to meet deadlines. Without advising ownership, they chose the latter, installing a $40 consumer-grade network switch in a utility closet to extend their cable reach.

This quick fix was never noted in any building systems documentation. Through the years, as staff turned over, knowledge of the switch's existence disappeared entirely. It became an invisible part of the building's digital infrastructure—a ghost in the system.

The building systems operated normally until about five years later—one year after the property was traded to new owners. That's when the undocumented switch failed, creating a cascading failure point. The failure of this switch knocked out all downstream systems. Security cameras went dark, door access controls failed, and unauthorized individuals gained access to restricted parts of the building. Tenants were understandably frustrated and concerned about their safety.

This situation illustrates a fundamental breakdown in digital infrastructure management. While the original owner had paid for a proper digital infrastructure design, the operations team failed to enforce its use. Both construction deadlines and communication gaps likely contributed to shortcuts being taken. Established protocols were circumvented, and operations staff inherited a system with hidden vulnerabilities. What began as an "unknown unknown"—a problem no one knew existed—became a "known unknown" when systems failed but no one could identify why.

OpticWise was able to identify the rogue network problem for the new owners. The original decision to save time and money with a $40 switch from The Home Depot led to weeks of system outages, extensive troubleshooting, and emergency repairs, all at significant cost. What should have been a proper $500 to $1,000 installation—becoming part of the managed digital infrastructure—developed into a much more expensive problem costing more than $20,000, not to mention the impact on tenant satisfaction and building security.

Just months after this incident, a similar situation nearly played out at another property when contractors mistakenly ran 10 percent of the network cables to an incorrect utility closet during construction. But this time, the proper communication channels were in place. The issue was identified and corrected immediately. Though the OpticWise team was able to integrate the mistake into existing digital infrastructure designs, rectifying it still required a five-figure expense. The difference was that rather than implementing a quick fix and hoping for the best, team members spoke up when they noticed something wasn't right.

These incidents reinforce a crucial lesson: Digital infrastructure isn't just about connecting systems—it's about connecting people. When teams communicate effectively, especially during construction, they can avoid the temptation of playing through the pain. Temporary solutions—the Band-Aids, braces, and painkillers—might mitigate things momentarily, but without proper intervention, these complications can become permanent problems.

Generally, the best play is stopping to address an issue properly, even if it means a short-term delay. Ultimately, doing things right the first time is always less painful than dealing with the consequences of shortcuts.

APPENDIX G

Sample Project Plan

C hapter 4 advised you to pick three initial "plays" that will set you on the path to data-driven success. Once you have selected your initial three plays, it's time to move from strategy to action by making a detailed project plan. This sample project plan will guide you in your efforts.

Although this example uses Vance and Vicki to explain the generation and use of such a plan, it is closely aligned with real numbers from an actual OpticWise project. It reveals how VRE might build a comprehensive framework to begin a data-driven transformation on their first greenfield project, "Greenfield Alpha."

The plan accounts for their existing team structure, current challenges, and future aspirations while providing clear objectives and accountability measures. The actual results exceeded the objectives listed here.

Victors Real Estate Group
Greenfield Alpha Net Operating
Income Improvement Project Plan

OBJECTIVES (SMART)

At Greenfield Alpha property (600 apartment units):

- Increase annual NOI by at least $465,000, as follows:
  - Reduce non-personnel annual operating expenses by a minimum of $110,000
  - Increase net income from technology services by a minimum of $355,000
  - Reduce CapEx build costs by a minimum of $450,000

PLAYERS/STAKEHOLDERS

- Executive sponsors: Vance and Vicki (VRE leadership)
- Technical partners: Dave and Kaylie (OpticWise)
- Key personnel:
  - Kevin (building engineer)
  - Property management team
  - Procurement team
  - Maintenance staff
- External partners:
  - Data science consultants
  - Equipment vendors
  - Services vendors
  - Utility vendors

DIGITAL AND PHYSICAL INFRASTRUCTURE

- Hardware requirements:
  - Resilient, centralized digital infrastructure connected to all of the following
  - Various IoT sensors for desired data inputs
  - Smart meters for all utility systems
  - Sensors for occupancy detection

- Environmental sensors (temperature, humidity)
- Network infrastructure upgrades vs. historical designs
- Core computing devices for real-time data processing
- Secure, mobile, private, property-wide connectivity platform
- Software requirements:
  - Data lake platform
  - Analytics dashboard
  - Operations systems: building automation systems, security systems, etc.
  - User-facing platform(s)

DATA INPUT SOURCES

- Water consumption metrics
- Energy usage data by location and consumption system
- Occupancy sensors
- Weather data feeds
- Building automation system data
- Historical utility bills
- Time-of-use utility billing data
- Environmental sensors

DATA OUTPUT

- Expected insights:
  - Real-time utility usage patterns
  - Consumption anomalies
  - Peak usage periods
  - Weather impact correlations
  - Occupancy-based optimization opportunities
  - Preventive maintenance indicators
  - Cost-saving opportunities
- Success metrics:
  - Annual NOI increase of $465,000 from:

continued

- Minimum 15 percent reduction in total utility costs
- Minimum 10 percent improvement in insurance premiums
- Minimum $350-per-door increased annual NOI from technology services
- Reduce CapEx build costs by $450,000:
  - Enhanced tenant satisfaction scores
  - Improved tenant retention rates

AI TOOLS AND HYPOTHESIS

- Tools:
  - Machine learning for:
    - Predictive analytics for usage forecasting
    - Anomaly detection algorithms
    - Optimization algorithms for resource allocation
- Hypotheses:
  - Blending occupancy data with utility usage will reveal optimization opportunities.
  - Weather pattern correlation will enable predictive HVAC adjustments.
  - AI-driven analytics will identify waste and inefficiencies.
  - Real-time monitoring will enable faster response to anomalies.
- Goal: Target initial focus on water consumption (proven 30 percent reduction potential) and expand to electrical and gas energy usage.

TIMELINE/GO LIVE

- Phase 1 (pre-construction):
  - Infrastructure assessment
  - Digital infrastructure detailed design
  - Hardware specification
  - Team training on new design strategies

- Phase 2 (construction):
  - Digital infrastructure wiring installation
  - Hardware procurement
  - Hardware installation
  - Property management (specifically leasing) training
  - Initial AI model training
  - Go live processes
  - Systems functional
- Phase 3 (regular reviews):
  - Optimization
  - Results measurement
  - Portfolio-wide rollout planning
  - System integration enhancements
  - Data validations and health checks

RESPONSIBILITY AND ACCOUNTABILITY MATRIX

- Strategic oversight:
  - Vance and Vicki: Final approval authority
  - Dave and Kaylie: Strategic guidance and technical oversight
- Technical implementation:
  - OpticWise team
    - Systems connected and collecting data
    - Digital infrastructure architecture and operation
    - User support
  - Data science team
    - Data lake maintenance
    - Analytics
    - AI implementation/operation
  - Procurement team: Supplier/vendor negotiations and contracting
  - Maintenance team: Infrastructure support

continued

- Operational execution:
    - Kevin: Day-to-day operations and system monitoring
    - Property management: Position technology services to tenant prospects
    - Maintenance team: Hardware (physical systems) maintenance
- Reporting structure:
    - Weekly: Technical team updates
    - Monthly: Stakeholder progress reviews
    - Quarterly: Executive and partner performance reviews
- Risk management:
    - Data security protocols
    - System redundancy plans
    - Change management strategies
    - Tenant communication plan
    - Compliance monitoring

Note: This plan is iterative and will be adjusted based on initial results and learnings from the pilot implementation.

Remember, You're the General Manager: A Cautionary Tale

n professional sports, the general manager (GM) sets the vision, makes the key personnel decisions, and ensures everyone executes the game plan. Star players might dazzle on the field, but it's the GM who builds the complete team and keeps everyone aligned with the long-term strategy.

The same principle applies to commercial real estate—particularly when it comes to digital infrastructure projects. When owners forget they're the ones in charge, even the best-designed plays can fall apart during execution.

A recent, actual development project (we'll call it the BlueSky Project) illustrates this principle perfectly. This greenfield project had all the makings of a championship property. The owners had engaged top consultants to design an optimized digital infrastructure that would serve as the backbone for all building systems. The design was elegant and efficient—calling for three strategically placed network closets and carefully mapped access point locations to provide comprehensive coverage while minimizing costs.

However, as construction progressed, the owners took a hands-off approach, essentially letting their contractors "call their own plays." It was like a GM had disappeared during training camp, leaving position coaches to make whatever changes they wanted to the playbook. The results were predictably chaotic for the BlueSky Project.

The engineering firm decided to act like a star player who needed to answer to no one. They improvised and unilaterally expanded the number of network closets from three to twelve. They also specified higher-grade cabling than necessary—the equivalent of insisting on premium equipment when standard gear would perform just as well.

Meanwhile, the installation contractor deviated from the carefully planned access point locations, laying out access points on a grid and creating coverage gaps that would require expensive fixes.

Most concerning, various contractors began installing standalone networks rather than connecting to the digital backbone as designed. Imagine a basketball team where each player decided to run their own plays instead of working within the designed offense. Just as that approach leads to inefficient, fragmented gameplay, these independent networks created unnecessary complexity and reduced operational efficiency.

The financial impact was staggering—over $235,000 in unnecessary CapEx costs from extra network closets, premium cable upgrades, unnecessary labor charges, and additional equipment needed to fix the network issues.

But the real damage went beyond immediate costs. Instead of one optimized digital infrastructure, the property ended up with multiple disconnected networks that would make it harder to collect and leverage data effectively. Essentially, the property owner had a team full of talented players who couldn't execute coordinated plays because they had never learned or wanted to work together.

The BlueSky Project offers crucial lessons for property owners. First, staying in the game matters. Just as a GM doesn't disappear after draft day, owners need to maintain active oversight throughout construction. You can't just design the plays—you need to make sure they're being executed properly.

Second, never forget who's in charge. You can build around great contractors, just as teams build around star players, but don't let them run the show. Unless given clear direction and oversight, contractors and vendors, like players, may naturally optimize for their own convenience and interests, particularly when faced with looming deadlines. Being "hands-off" doesn't make you look sophisticated or nonchalant—it signals that nobody's really in charge.

Third, lay the vision out for your design and construction teams. Don't assume they understand; you need to share and explain this vision. If others don't know your goals, they will likely default to what they know—the status quo. And for a championship owner, the CRE status quo is not acceptable.

Finally, keep your eye on the championship. Short-term contractor convenience shouldn't compromise long-term operational goals. Every decision about infrastructure design and installation impacts how efficiently your property will operate for years to come. Slight deviations can have major impacts on overall system performance.

Here are some important takeaways:

- Active oversight isn't micromanagement—it's leadership.
- Trust your contractors' expertise, but verify that their decisions align with your strategy.
- Continuously repeat your vision and goals to your design and construction teams.
- Remember that today's construction choices determine tomorrow's operational capabilities.
- Stay focused on the end goal: an efficient, integrated digital infrastructure that positions your property for sustained success.

Remember, you're the GM. Your contractors might be executing the plays, but you're responsible for making sure those plays serve your long-term strategy. Don't delegate that responsibility—embrace it. After all, when a team fails to perform, nobody asks why the position coaches didn't do better. They ask, "What on earth was the GM thinking?"

Make sure you have an answer.

For Additional Support

OPTIC WISE

BUILDING INTELLIGENCE

The next revolution in commercial real estate is what we call OpticWise Building Intelligence—the ability to use property operating data to strategically increase NOI.

And this next wave requires complete control of your data and digital infrastructures.

Only when you own and control your digital infrastructure can you capture and fully utilize your building's data to aggregate it, analyze it, apply it—and ultimately, monetize it.

Own and control your digital infrastructure.

Own, control, and leverage your data.

https://www.OpticWise.com

888-OpticWise (888-678-4294)

info@opticwise.com

THE RESILIENCE GUY

EXECUTIVE COACHING

Bill Douglas is known as the ResilienceGuy.

He's had very interesting and challenging life experiences, including two near-death experiences and a life-changing medical diagnosis, resulting in his mantra: Lift is a GIFT!

He coaches executives and entrepreneurs to live more, own your time, and make a bigger impact without compromising on wealth, health, or relationships.

Learn more about Bill, his principles, his purpose, and his pursuit of unique experiences, as well as his methodology, which revolves around health, wellness, and resilience in every factor of one's life.

https://www.ResilienceGuy.com

Acknowledgments

As a team, we'd all like to thank the remarkable Greenleaf and Fast Company team (Justin Branch, Madison Johnson, Maxine Marshall, Erin Pedigo, Brian Welch, Madelyn Myers, and Gwen Cunningham), and Amy Dorta McIlwaine at FoolProof Editing, for your editorial and business acumen; John van der Woude for your excellent cover design; and Seth Konkey for your critical feedback on an early draft.

Bill

First and foremost, I am grateful to and for my sons, JB and Britt. You two are my purpose in life. I am insanely proud of the men you've chosen to become and the positive impact you will continue to have on this world.

To my mom, Tish, for setting my foundation very early in life of resilience and the desire to always be learning.

To my ELAN forum (Andre, Cam, Dan, Matt, and Scott), who have ridden through nearly two decades of every aspect of life alongside me with encouragement, support, and guidance.

To Bill Weiss and Tom Noonan for extraordinary business and leadership counsel and deep friendships over the decades.

To all of the OpticWise team, who eagerly take on any and all challenges that life, business, and clients bring to us.

And to Julie, who steadfastly stands with me as I dream, discuss, overanalyze, and execute ideas into reality—your abiding patience and support are priceless.

Drew

Team efforts are amazing, and when you've got a great team, possible is everything (yes, that's worded correctly!). To my family team—Debbie, Hudson, and Beckham—I love you deeply. Without your care, coverage, understanding, acceptance, and encouragement, OpticWise would not exist. With God as the author, our family inspires creativity in such a unique and amazing way. And that creativity has fueled the beyond-the-box thinking that has put OpticWise in the position it's in today.

To Mom and Dad, your never-bending, faithful support and core belief in me has made molehills out of so many would-be mountains in my life.

To some incredibly talented friends—DK, JR, Eddie, Ferney, Shawn K., Shawn A., and Derek—your ingenious and continuous contributions are forever imprinted directly into OpticWise's identity.

And to my original technical support team—Roger, Oliver, Reed, Hudson, and Deborah—your creative commitment to OpticWise and the GHS mission has been relentless. Scaling this business would not have been possible without you.

Ryan

I am deeply grateful to a few groups of professional collaborators who made this book possible.

First and foremost, Bill Douglas, Drew Hall, and Karen Freitag—thank you for inviting me into OpticWise's visionary work. You have been incredible teachers and remarkable cowriters throughout this journey.

Second, Carol Enoch of Enoch & Company, who welcomed me into both her team and the OpticWise project with deep real estate wisdom, and Angela Gerber at The Marketing Apothecary, whose expertise and generous friendship have brought so much joy to working in CRE.

Third, the core Mindblue team (Nick Gerger, Jenna Hatch, and Pam Goble) and the Irrational Labs team (Kristen Berman, Brad Goodwin, and every brilliant person at the organization)—who have made so much meaningful work possible across education and business spaces over the years.

Saving the best for last, to my wife, Nicole, and daughter, Téa—you are the heart of every great story in my life. Thank you for your endless support and patience during the long writing days. I love you both.

Glossary

INTRODUCTION

artificial intelligence (AI): Computer systems that can perform tasks that normally require human intelligence—this includes natural language processing (NLP), robotic process automation (RPA), and machine learning (ML). For more information, see appendix C.

commercial real estate (CRE): Properties used for income-generating business purposes.

digital infrastructure: The hardware, software, and networks that run a building's technology systems.

hardware: Physical technology equipment like computers, sensors, and cables.

heating, ventilation, and air-conditioning (HVAC): Systems that control indoor temperature and air quality.

internet service provider (ISP): Company that provides internet connectivity services.

net operating income (NOI): The net income a CRE property generates (revenues minus expenses).

return on investment (ROI): The profitability or benefit gained compared with the cost.

smart building: Property using networked sensors and automation to optimize operations.

CHAPTER 1

brownfield project: Upgrading or renovating an existing building.

building automation systems (BAS): Centralized network of connected devices to monitor and control various building systems.

building management systems (BMS): Computer-based system to monitor and control a building's systems. A BMS is a more comprehensive system that includes a BAS.

business intelligence (BI): Tools and methods for analyzing business data to make better decisions.

capital expenditure (CapEx): One-time expenses for buying major equipment or assets.

Data & Digital Infrastructure Audit (DDIA): Assessment of a property's technology systems and data.

data and digital infrastructure domains: The six core technology categories (or "domains") of a property's digital ecosystem include network infrastructure and IoT; security, access control, and risk management; energy, environmental management, and sustainability; property operations and tenant experience; financial and asset management; and data aggregation and analytics. Each domain includes both software (digital) and hardware (physical) components that work together to enable smart building operations.

data lake: Large repository storing raw data in its original format.

data warehouse: Storage system for structured, filtered data.

greenfield project: New construction project starting from scratch.

Internet of Things (IoT): Connected devices and sensors that collect and share data.

operating expenses (OpEx): Ongoing costs to run a business from day to day.

CHAPTER 2

data repository: Central location where data is stored and managed.

digital backbone: Core technology infrastructure connecting building systems.

key performance indicator (KPI): Important metrics used to measure performance.

pull system: System where data must be requested to be retrieved.

push system: Technology that automatically sends data to a central location.

unified digital infrastructure: A single integrated network connecting all building systems.

CHAPTER 3

application programming interface (API): A way for different software systems to communicate and share data.

California Consumer Privacy Act (CCPA): Privacy law protecting California residents' personal data.

General Data Protection Privacy Regulation (GDPR): European Union privacy law protecting personal data.

user experience (UX): The overall experience a user has when interacting with a product, system, or service.

webhook: A lightweight, automated way for applications to communicate with each other via HTTP.

CHAPTER 4

blended data: Information combined from multiple systems or sources.

single data source: Information from just one system or component.

time-of-use billing: Utility rates that vary based on the time of day.

CHAPTER 5

bidirectional data flow: Data that can be both sent and received between systems.

input command: Instruction sent/received to control systems.

output data: Information sent/received to control systems.

systems interoperability: Ability of different systems to work together and share data.

CHAPTER 6

performance-enhancing data and systems (PEDS): Using data and technology to improve performance.

portfolio optimization: Strategic improvements across multiple properties.

scalable system: Technology that can grow with the organization.

About the Authors

BILL DOUGLAS is the CEO of OpticWise, a cutting-edge company that provides data and digital infrastructure solutions for the commercial real estate industry. With over three decades of entrepreneurial experience, Bill has established himself as a leading expert in technology empowerment in various industries. His innovative approaches have enabled companies to create wholly owned digital ecosystems that drive revenue growth and improve operational efficiency. Bill is a lifetime entrepreneur, leading multiple companies onto the Inc. 5000 list. A member of *Marquis Who's Who* and a US patent holder, he has received multiple awards, including "Best Entrepreneurs to Watch" and "Top 10 Business Leaders Making a Difference." Bill holds a bachelor's of mechanical engineering degree from the Georgia Institute of Technology and is a graduate of the Massachusetts Institute of Technology's Enterprise Forum Entrepreneurial Masters Program, along with MIT's AI: Implications for Business Strategy Program. Known as the "ResilienceGuy," Bill also coaches executives and entrepreneurs to *live more, own your time*, and *make a bigger impact without compromising on wealth, health, or relationships.*

https://www.linkedin.com/in/billdouglas

https://www.resilienceguy.com

Author photo by Jen Honeycutt Photography

DREW HALL is the founder and chief systems architect at OpticWise. He brings a wealth of experience in designing expansive, high-performance networks for demanding clients in both the commercial and federal sectors, through professional engagements with IBM and the US Department of the Interior. Drew's expertise lies in extending and adapting advanced technologies to meet the unique needs of the commercial real estate industry. Under his technical leadership, OpticWise has developed innovative solutions that empower property owners and investors to unlock the full potential of their data and digital infrastructure assets. In addition to the overtly technical world, Drew is also actively involved in improvisational comedy, both as an executive team corporate trainer and as an actor in team performances. He swears by the application of improv comedy in building healthy business teams: the skills of active listening, collaboration, owning your choices, and the "yes, and" mindset. Drew holds a bachelor's of science degree in computer science from Baylor University.

https://www.linkedin.com/in/drewhall33/